"The life of Jesus of Naz... 2,000 years later. *More* ...

JOHN ORTBERG
Author and pastor o...

"I found the original *More Than a Carpenter* persuasive when I was an atheist; you'll find this updated and expanded version even more compelling."

LEE STROBEL
Author of The Case for Christ *and* The Case for the Real Jesus

"In a day when rational thought seems to be in short supply, *More Than a Carpenter* is an antidote for the truth vacuum of our times."

CHUCK KLEIN
Youth and campus ministry advocate
Campus Crusade for Christ

"I loved this book when it first came out, to help me share Christ with my friends. I plan on using this new edition with many people I love!"

JOHN ELDREDGE
Author of Wild at Heart *and* Walking with God

"A masterful blend of scholarship and readability . . . that will appeal to both teens and adults alike."

GREG STIER
President and CEO, Dare 2 Share Ministries

"Like millions of others, *More Than a Carpenter* helped lead me to Jesus Christ. I am excited to see how God will use this book to change lives."

MARK DRISCOLL
Pastor, Mars Hill Church

"This unapologetic search for truth challenges a new generation to take a closer look at Jesus."

ANDY STANLEY
Senior pastor, North Point Community Church

"Josh and Sean McDowell present the claims of Christ in a clear and convincing way."

DR. JOHN TOWNSEND
Psychologist, speaker, and coauthor of **Boundaries**

"Josh and Sean have succeeded in improving a classic. More than a good read, it's a game changer."

WAYNE RICE
Cofounder of Youth Specialties

"Even more powerful and relevant for this generation."

JIM BURNS, PhD
President of HomeWord; author of **Creating an Intimate Marriage** *and* **Confident Parenting**

"After reading *More Than a Carpenter*, skeptics, spiritual seekers, and people of any faith will find reasons to believe in the claims of Jesus and to follow him."

ALEC HILL
President, InterVarsity Christian Fellowship USA

"The chapter dealing with the exclusivity of Jesus is the best treatment of this subject that I have read."

ALEX MCFARLAND
President, Southern Evangelical Seminary and the Veritas School of Apologetics

"Whether you are a longtime Christian or not sure about what you believe, you will be impacted by *More Than a Carpenter*."

REBECCA ST. JAMES
Singer, author, actress

More Than a Carpenter

josh mcdowell
sean mcdowell

Tyndale House Publishers
Carol Stream, Illinois

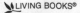LIVING BOOKS®

Visit Tyndale online at www.tyndale.com.

Visit Tyndale Momentum online at www.tyndalemomentum.com.

Tyndale, Tyndale's quill logo, *Tyndale Momentum*, and the Tyndale Momentum logo are registered trademarks of Tyndale House Ministries. Tyndale Momentum is a nonfiction imprint of Tyndale House Publishers, Carol Stream, Illinois.

More Than a Carpenter

For information about special discounts for bulk purchases, please contact Tyndale House Publishers at csresponse@tyndale.com, or call 1-800-323-9400.

Library of Congress Cataloging-in-Publication Data

McDowell, Josh.
  More than a carpenter / Josh McDowell, Sean McDowell. — [New, rev. ed.].
    p. cm.
  Includes bibliographical references.
  ISBN 978-1-4143-2627-6 (sc : alk. paper)
  ISBN 978-1-4143-3380-9 (sc multi-packs)
  1. Jesus Christ—Person and offices. I. McDowell, Sean. II. Title.
BT203.M3386 2009
232—dc22   2008054623

Printed in the United States of America

27   26   25   24   23   22   21
22   21   20   19   18   17   16

To Dick and Charlotte Day,
whose lives have always reflected that
Jesus was more than a carpenter

Contents

Preface

When I first sat down in 1976 with twelve legal pads, forty-eight hours of free time, and a *lot* of coffee to write the book that would become *More Than a Carpenter*, I did so hoping that it would help followers of Jesus to respond to questions about their faith, and inspire spiritual seekers to honestly investigate the claims of Jesus. I never dreamed that the story of my personal journey from skepticism to belief would ultimately sell more than fifteen million copies, be translated into nearly one hundred languages, and inspire readers around the world to take a closer, deeper look at the possibility of faith. I continue to be honored and humbled each time someone tells me that my book made a difference in his or her life.

Yet I also continue to be struck by how much has happened in the world since *More Than a Carpenter* first released. Discoveries have been made (and continue to be made) which shed light on the historicity of Jesus Christ. "New Atheists" have entered the popular culture with books proclaiming the end of faith and the downfall of God. And while today's generation faces a whole host of new issues and choices, they also continue to confront the age-old questions: Who is Jesus? What proof is there that he was the son of God? And even if it were true, what difference would it make to my life?

Based on all this, I decided it was time to give *More Than a Carpenter* a makeover for the twenty-first century. So I invited my son, Sean, a well-known speaker, teacher, and writer on apologetics and the Bible, to update the book with me. Sean brought his strong academic credentials (a double master's degree in philosophy and theology) to the table, along with his own experience as an author, providing a welcome perspective on postmodern faith. The two of us worked together to create a brand-new chapter, revised material, discussion questions, and a fresh look. The result is a new edition of *More Than a Carpenter* that nonetheless retains its original hard-hitting examination of the facts and unapologetic search for truth.

It is my profound desire and Sean's that this book will have a transformational impact on a new generation of people on a quest for spiritual clarity.

—*JM*

CHAPTER 1

My Story

THIRTEENTH-CENTURY PHILOSOPHER THOMAS AQUINAS writes: "There is within every soul a thirst for happiness and meaning." I first began to feel this thirst when I was a teenager. I wanted to be happy. I wanted my life to have meaning. I became hounded by those three basic questions that haunt every human life: Who am I? Why am I here? Where am I going? I wanted answers, so as a young student, I started searching for them.

Where I was brought up, everyone seemed to be into religion, so I thought I might find my answers in being religious. I got into church 150 percent. I went every time the doors opened—morning, afternoon, or evening. But I must have picked the wrong church because I felt worse inside it than I did outside. From my upbringing on a farm in Michigan I inherited a rural practicality that says when something doesn't work, get rid of it. So I chucked religion.

Then I thought that education might have the answers

to my quest for meaning, so I enrolled in a university. I soon became the most unpopular student among the professors. I would buttonhole them in their offices and badger them for answers to my questions. When they saw me coming, they would turn out the lights, pull down the shades, and lock their doors. You can learn many things at a university, but I didn't find the answers I was seeking. Faculty members and my fellow students had just as many problems, frustrations, and unanswered questions as I did.

One day on campus I saw a student wearing a T-shirt that read, "Don't follow me, I'm lost." That's how everyone in the university seemed to me. Education, I decided, was not the answer.

What Do You Think?

Do you agree with philosopher Thomas Aquinas that "There is within every soul a thirst for happiness and meaning"?

I began to think maybe I could find happiness and meaning in prestige. I would find a noble cause, dedicate myself to it, and in the process, become well known on campus. The people with the most prestige in the university were the student leaders, who also controlled the purse strings. So I got elected to various student offices. It was a heady experience to know everyone on campus, to make important decisions, to spend the university's money getting the speakers I wanted and the students' money for throwing parties.

But the thrill of prestige wore off like everything else I had tried. I would wake up on Monday morning, usually with a headache because of the night before, dreading to face another five miserable days. I endured Monday through Friday, living only for the partying nights

2

of Friday, Saturday, and Sunday. Then on Monday the meaningless cycle would begin all over again.

I didn't let on that my life was meaningless; I was too proud for that. Everyone thought I was the happiest man on campus. They never suspected that my happiness was a sham. It depended on my circumstances. If things were going great for me, I felt great. When things were going lousy, I felt lousy. I just didn't let it show.

Everyone thought I was the happiest man on campus. But the life I was living was hell.

I was like a boat out in the ocean, tossed back and forth by the waves. I had no rudder—no direction or control. But I couldn't find anyone living any other way. I couldn't find anyone who could tell me how to live differently. I was frustrated. No, it was worse than that. There's a strong term that describes the life I was living: hell.

About that time I noticed a small group of people—eight students and two faculty members—who seemed different from the others. They seemed to know who they were and where they were going. And they had convictions. It is refreshing to find people with convictions, and I like to be around them. I admire people who believe in something and take a stand for it, even if I don't agree with their beliefs.

It was clear to me that these people had something I didn't have. They were disgustingly

What Do You Think?

Do you like being around people with convictions? What makes it an invigorating experience? What makes it a frustrating one?

happy. And their happiness didn't ride up and down with the circumstances of university life; it was constant. They appeared to possess an inner source of joy, and I wondered where it came from.

Something else about these people caught my attention—their attitudes and actions toward each other. They genuinely loved each other—and not only each other, but the people outside their group as well. And I don't mean they just talked about love; they got involved in people's lives, helping them with their needs and problems. It was all totally foreign to me, yet I was strongly attracted to it.

Like most people, when I see something I want but don't have, I start trying to figure out a way to get it. So I decided to make friends with these intriguing people.

A couple of weeks later I sat around a table in the student union talking to some of the members of this group. The conversation turned to the topic of God. I was pretty skeptical and insecure about this subject, so I put on a big front. I leaned back in my chair, acting as if I couldn't care less.

"Christianity, ha! That's for unthinking weaklings, not intellectuals." Of course, under all the bluster I really wanted what these people had.

"Christianity, ha!" I blustered. "That's for unthinking weaklings, not intellectuals." Of course, under all the bluster I really wanted what these people had, but my pride didn't want them to know the aching urgency of my need. The subject bothered me, but I couldn't let go of it. So I turned to one of the students, a good-looking woman (I used to think all Christians were ugly), and I said, "Tell me, why are you so different from all the other students and faculty on this campus? What changed your life?"

Without hesitation or embarrassment she looked me straight in the eye, deadly serious, and uttered two words I never expected to hear in an intelligent discussion on a university campus: "Jesus Christ."

"Jesus Christ?" I snapped. "Oh, for God's sake, don't give me that kind of garbage. I'm fed up with religion. I'm fed up with the church. I'm fed up with the Bible."

Immediately she shot back, "I didn't say *religion*, I said Jesus Christ!" She pointed out something I had never known: Christianity is not a religion. Religion is

Christianity is not a religion. Religion is humans trying to work their way to God through good works. Christianity is God coming to men and women through Jesus Christ.

humans trying to work their way to God through good works. Christianity is God coming to men and women through Jesus Christ.

I wasn't buying it. Not for a minute. Taken aback by the young woman's courage and conviction, I apologized for my attitude. "But I'm sick and tired of religion and religious people," I explained. "I don't want anything to do with them."

Then my new friends issued a challenge I couldn't believe. They challenged me to make a rigorous, intellectual examination of the claims of Jesus Christ—that he is God's Son; that he inhabited a human body and lived among real men and women; that he died on the cross for the sins of humanity; that he was buried and was resurrected three days later; and that he is still alive and can change a person's life even today.

I thought this challenge was a joke. Everyone with any sense knew that Christianity was based on a myth.

What Do You Think?
How would you define religion?

I thought that only a walking idiot could believe the myth that Christ came back from the dead. I used to wait for Christians to speak out in the classroom so I could tear them up one side and down the other. I thought that if a Christian had a brain cell, it would die of loneliness.

But I accepted my friends' challenge, mostly out of spite to prove them wrong. I was convinced the Christian story would not stand up to evidence. I was a prelaw student, and I knew something about evidence. I would investigate the claims of Christianity thoroughly and come back and knock the props out from under their sham religion.

If I could show that the Bible was historically untrustworthy, then I could show that Christianity was a fantasy made up by wishful religious dreamers.

I decided to start with the Bible. I knew that if I could uncover indisputable evidence that the Bible is an unreliable record, the whole of Christianity would crumble. Sure, Christians could show me that their own book said Christ was born of a virgin, that he performed miracles, and that he rose from the dead. But what good was that? If I could show that the Bible was historically untrustworthy, then I could show that Christianity was a fantasy made up by wishful religious dreamers.

I took the challenge seriously. I spent months in research. I even dropped out of school for a time to study in the historically rich libraries of Europe. And I found evidence. Evidence in abundance. Evidence I would not have believed had I not seen it with my own eyes. Finally I could come to only one conclusion: If I were to remain intellectually honest, I had to admit that the Old and New Testament documents were some of the most reliable writings in all of antiquity. And if they were reliable, what about this man Jesus, whom I had dismissed as a mere carpenter in an out-of-the-way town in a tiny oppressed country, a man who had gotten caught up in his own visions of grandeur?

I found evidence. Evidence in abundance. I had to admit that the Old and New Testament documents were some of the most reliable writings in all of antiquity.

I had to admit that Jesus Christ was *more* than a carpenter. He was all he claimed to be.

Not only did my research turn me around intellectually, but it also answered the three questions that started me on my quest for happiness and meaning. But as Paul Harvey says, that's the "rest of the story." I will tell you all about that at the end of this book. First, I want to share with you the core of what I

What Do You Think?
If God did become man, what would be the best way for him to communicate to his creation?

7

learned in my months of research so that you, too, may see that Christianity is not a myth, not the fantasy of wishful dreamers, not a hoax played on the simpleminded. It is rock-solid truth. And I guarantee that when you come to terms with that truth, you will be on the threshold of finding the answers to those three questions: Who am I? What is my purpose? What is my destiny?

CHAPTER 2

What Makes Jesus So Different?

SOMETIME AFTER MY DISCOVERIES ABOUT THE BIBLE AND Christianity, I was riding in a cab in London and happened to mention something about Jesus to the driver. Immediately he retorted, "I don't like to discuss religion, especially Jesus." I couldn't help but notice the similarity of his reaction to my own when the young Christian woman told me that Jesus Christ had changed her life. The very name Jesus seems to bother people. It embarrasses them, makes them angry, or makes them want to change the subject. You can talk about God, and people don't necessarily get upset, but mention Jesus, and people want to stop the conversation. Why don't the names of Buddha, Muhammad, or Confucius offend people the way the name of Jesus does?

I think the reason is that these other religious leaders didn't claim to be God. That is the big difference between Jesus and the others. It didn't take long for people who knew Jesus to realize that this carpenter from Nazareth was making astounding claims about himself. It became clear that those claims were identifying him as more than just a prophet or teacher. He was obviously making claims to deity. He was presenting himself as the only avenue to salvation and the only source of forgiveness of sins—things they knew that only God could claim.

For many people today Jesus' claim to be the Son of God is just too exclusive. In our pluralistic culture, it is too narrow and smacks of religious bigotry. We don't want to believe it. Yet the issue is not what we want to believe, but rather, who did Jesus claim to be? And is his claim true?

> **What Do You Think?**
> *Jesus said he was the Son of God. Why is that a problem for many people? Why is it less offensive to talk about God than Jesus?*

That's what I went to find out when I took up the gauntlet from my university friends.

I started by exploring all I could about the New Testament documents to see what they could tell us about this claim. I began to analyze the phrase "the deity of Christ" to see just what exactly was meant in the claim that Jesus Christ is God. Augustus H. Strong, former president of Rochester Theological Seminary, in his *Systematic Theology* defines God as the "infinite and perfect spirit in whom all things have their source, support, and end."[1] This definition of God is adequate not only for Christians but also for all theists, including Muslims and Jews. Theism teaches that God is personal and that the universe was planned and created by him. God sustains and rules it in the present. But Christian theism adds an additional note to the definition: God became incarnate as Jesus of Nazareth.

The words *Jesus Christ* are not a first and last name; they are actually a name and a title. The name Jesus is derived from the Greek form of the name *Jeshua* or Joshua, meaning "Jehovah-Savior" or "the Lord saves." The title Christ is derived from the Greek word for Messiah (or the Hebrew *Mashiach*, see Daniel 9:26) and means "anointed one."

Two offices, king and priest, are indicated in the use of the title *Christ*. The title affirms Jesus as the promised priest and king of Old Testament prophecies. This affirmation is crucial to a proper understanding about Jesus and Christianity.

> **The name Jesus means "Jehovah-Savior" or "the Lord saves." The title Christ is derived from the Greek word for Messiah and means "anointed one."**

The New Testament clearly presents Christ as God. Most of the names applied to Christ are such that they could properly be applied only to one who was God. For example, Jesus is called God in the statement "while we look forward with hope to that wonderful day when the glory of our great God and Savior, Jesus Christ, will be revealed" (Titus 2:13; see also John 1:1; Romans 9:5; Hebrews 1:8; 1 John 5:20-21). The Scriptures attribute characteristics to him that can be true only of God. They present Jesus as being self-existent (see John 1:2; 8:58; 17:5; 17:24); omnipresent (see Matthew 18:20; 28:20); omniscient (see Matthew 17:22-27; John 4:16-18; 6:64); omnipotent (see Matthew 8:26-27; Luke 4:38-41; 7:14-15; 8:24-25; Revelation 1:8); and possessing eternal life (see 1 John 5:11-12, 20).

Jesus received honor and worship that only God should receive. In a confrontation with Satan, Jesus said, "For the

Scriptures say, 'You must worship the LORD your God and serve only him' " (Matthew 4:10). Yet Jesus received worship as God (see Matthew 14:33; 28:9) and sometimes even claimed to be worthy of worship as God (see John 5:23; Hebrews 1:6; Revelation 5:8-14). Most of the early followers of Jesus were devout Jews who believed in one true God. They were monotheistic to the core, yet as the following examples show, they recognized him as God incarnate.

The Scriptures attribute characteristics to him that can be true only of God. Jesus received honor and worship that only God should receive.

Because of the apostle Paul's extensive rabbinical training, he would be an unlikely person to attribute deity to Jesus, to worship a man from Nazareth and call him Lord. But this is exactly what Paul did. He acknowledged Jesus as God when he said, "Feed and shepherd God's flock—his church, purchased with his own blood—over which the Holy Spirit has appointed you as elders" (Acts 20:28).

After Jesus asked his disciples who they thought he was, Simon Peter confessed, "You are the Messiah, the Son of the living God" (Matthew 16:16). Jesus responded to Peter's confession, not by correcting the man's conclusion, but by acknowledging its validity and source: "You are blessed, Simon son of John, because my Father in heaven has revealed this to you. You did not learn this from any human being" (Matthew 16:17).

Martha, a close friend of Jesus, said to him, "I have always believed you are the Messiah, the Son of God" (John 11:27). Then there is the plainspoken Nathanael, who didn't believe anything good could come out of Naza-reth. He admitted to Jesus, "Rabbi, you are the Son of God—the King of Israel!" (John 1:49). While the first Christian martyr, Stephen, was being stoned, he cried out and said, "Lord Jesus, receive my spirit" (Acts 7:59). The writer of the book of Hebrews calls Christ God when he writes, "To the Son he says, 'Your throne, O God, endures forever and ever' " (Hebrews 1:8).

Then, of course, we have Thomas, better known as "the doubter." (Perhaps he was a graduate student.) He said, "I won't believe it unless I see the nail wounds in his hands, put my fingers into them, and place my hand into the wound in his side" (John 20:25). I identify with Thomas. He was saying, "Look, not every day does someone raise himself from the dead or claim to be God incarnate. If you expect me to believe, I need evidence." Eight days later, after Thomas had expressed his doubts about Jesus to the other disciples, Jesus sud-denly appeared. "'Peace be with you,' he said. Then he said to Thomas, 'Put your finger here, and look at my hands. Put your hand into the wound in my

What Do You Think?

Would you consider yourself more of a Martha (always a believer) or a Thomas (a doubter) or a Nathanael (a cynic) in your attitudes about Jesus?

side. Don't be faithless any longer. Believe!' 'My Lord and my God!' Thomas exclaimed." (John 20:26-28). Jesus accepted Thomas's acknowledgment of him as God. He rebuked Thomas for his unbelief but not for his worship.

At this point a critic might interject that all these claims are from others about Christ, not from Christ about him-self. People who lived at the time of Christ misunderstood him as we misunderstand him today. They attributed deity to him, but he didn't really claim it for himself.

Well, when we delve deeper into the pages of the New Testament, we find that Christ did indeed make this claim. The references are abundant, and their meaning is plain. A businessman who scrutinized the Scriptures to verify whether or not Christ claimed to be God said, "Anyone who reads the New Testament and does not conclude that Jesus claimed to be divine would have to be as blind as a man standing outdoors on a clear day and saying he can't see the sun."

In the Gospel of John we have a confrontation between Jesus and a group of Jews. It was triggered by the fact that Jesus had cured a lame man on the Sabbath. (Jews were forbidden to do any work on the Sabbath.) "So the Jewish leaders began harassing Jesus for breaking the Sabbath rules. But Jesus replied, 'My Father is always working, and so am I.' So the Jewish leaders tried all the harder to find a way to kill him. For he not only broke the Sabbath, he called God his Father, thereby making himself equal with God" (John 5:16-18).

What Do You Think?

Why do you think the Jewish leaders were so enraged with Jesus after he healed on the Sabbath? Was it because he did it on a sacred day or something else?

You might say, "Look, Josh, I can't see how this proves anything. Jesus called God his Father. So what? All Christians call God their Father, but this doesn't mean they are claiming to be God." The Jews of Jesus' time heard in Jesus' words a meaning that is easily lost to us now. Whenever we study a document, we must take into account the language, the culture, and especially the person or persons the document addresses. In this case, the culture is Jewish, and the persons addressed are Jewish religious leaders. And something about what Jesus said really got under their skin. "So the Jewish leaders tried all the harder to find a way to kill him. For he not only broke the Sabbath, he called God his Father, thereby making himself equal with God" (John 5:18). What could he have said to cause such a drastic reaction? Let's look at the passage and see how the Jews understood Jesus' remarks more than two thousand years ago in their own culture.

You might say, "Jesus called God his Father. So what? All Christians call God their Father, but this doesn't mean they are claiming to be God."

Their problem was that Jesus said "*my* Father," not "*our* Father." By the rules of their language, Jesus' use of this phrase was a claim to be equal with God. The Jews did not refer to God as "my Father." Or if they did, they would always qualify the statement by adding the phrase "in heaven." However, Jesus did not add the phrase. He made a claim the Jews could not misinterpret when he called God "my Father."

To make matters worse, by the phrase "My Father is always working, and so am I," Jesus was putting his own activity on an equal plane with God's. Again the Jews understood that he was claiming to be God's Son. As a result, their hatred of Jesus grew. Until this point they had been seeking only to persecute him, but soon they began to plan to kill him.

Not only did Jesus claim equality with God as his Father, but he also asserted that he was one with the Father. During the Feast of the Dedication in Jerusalem, some of the other Jewish leaders approached Jesus and questioned him about whether he was the Christ. Jesus concluded his comments to them by saying, "The Father and I are one" (John 10:30). "Once again the people picked up stones to kill him. Jesus said, 'At my Father's direction I have done many good works. For which one are you going to stone me?'" (John 10:31-32).

One might wonder why the Jews reacted so strongly to what Jesus said about being one with the Father. The structure of the phrase in the Greek gives us an answer. A. T. Robertson, the foremost Greek scholar of his day, writes that in the Greek the word *one* in this passage is neuter, not masculine, and does not indicate one in person or purpose but rather one in "essence or nature." Robertson then adds, "This crisp statement is the climax of Christ's claims about the relation between the Father and himself [the Son]. They stir the Pharisees to uncontrollable anger."[2]

It is evident that in this statement the Jews clearly heard Jesus claiming to be God. Thus, Leon Morris, former principal of Ridley College, Melbourne, writes that

> the Jews could regard Jesus' word only as blasphemy, and they proceeded to take the judgment into their own hands. It was laid down in the Law that blasphemy was to be punished by stoning (see Leviticus 24:16). But these men were not allowing the due processes of law to take their course. They were not preparing an indictment so that the authorities could take the requisite action. In their fury they were preparing to be judges and executioners in one.[3]

The Jews threatened Jesus with stoning for "blasphemy," which tells us that they definitely understood his claim to be God. But, we may ask, did they stop to consider whether or not this claim was true?

Jesus continually spoke of himself as one in essence and nature with God. He boldly asserted, "If you knew me, you would also know my Father" (John 8:19). "For when you see me, you are seeing the one who sent me" (John 12:45). "Anyone who hates me also hates my Father" (John 15:23). "Everyone will honor the Son, just as they honor the Father. Anyone who does not honor the Son is certainly not honoring the Father who sent him" (John 5:23). These references definitely indicate that Jesus looked at himself as being more than just a man; he claimed to be equal with God.

What Do You Think?

The Jews wanted to stone Jesus for blasphemy. Was their own guilt over not believing him beginning to convict them? Or were they just jealous of his popularity?

Those who say that Jesus was just closer or more intimate with God than others need to consider his statement, "Anyone who does not honor the Son is certainly not honoring the Father who sent him."

While I was lecturing in a literature class at a university in West Virginia, a professor interrupted me and said that the only Gospel in which Jesus claimed to be God was John's Gospel, and it was the latest one written. He then asserted that Mark, the earliest Gospel, never once mentioned that Jesus claimed to be God. This man simply had not read Mark carefully.

In response I turned to Mark's Gospel, to a passage in which Jesus claimed to be able to forgive sins. "Seeing their faith, Jesus said to the paralyzed man, 'My child, your sins are forgiven'" (Mark 2:5; see also Luke 7:48-50). According to Jewish theology, only God could say such a thing; Isaiah 43:25 restricts forgiveness of sin to the prerogative of God alone. When the scribes heard Jesus forgiving the man's sins, they asked, "What is he saying? This is blasphemy! Only God can forgive sins!" (Mark 2:7). Jesus then asked which would be easier to say to a paralyzed man, "Your sins are forgiven" or "Stand up, pick up your mat, and walk"?

Those who say that Jesus was just more intimate with God than others need to consider his statement, "Anyone who does not honor the Son is certainly not honoring the Father who sent him."

According to *The Wycliffe Bible Commentary*, this is

> an unanswerable question. The statements are equally simple to pronounce; but to say either, with accompanying performance, requires divine power. An imposter, of course, in seeking to avoid detection, would find the former easier. Jesus proceeded to heal the illness that men might know that he had authority to deal with its cause.[4]

At this the religious leaders accused him of blasphemy. Lewis Sperry Chafer, founder and first president of Dallas Theological Seminary, writes that

> none on earth has either authority or right to forgive sin. None could forgive sin save the One against whom all have sinned. When Christ forgave

sin, as he certainly did, He was not exercising a human prerogative. Since none but God can forgive sins, it is conclusively demonstrated that Christ, since he forgave sins, is God.[5]

This concept of forgiveness bothered me for quite a while because I didn't understand it. One day in a philosophy class, answering a question about the deity of Christ, I quoted Mark 2:5. A graduate assistant challenged my conclusion that Christ's forgiveness of sin demonstrates his deity. He said that he could forgive people without the act's demonstrating any claim to be God. People do it all the time. As I pondered what the man was saying, the answer suddenly struck me. I knew why the religious leaders reacted so strongly against Christ. Yes, one can say, "I forgive you," but only if he is the one who has been sinned against. If you sin against me, I have the right to forgive you. But if you sin against someone else, I have no such right. The paralytic had not sinned against the man Jesus; the two men had never even seen each other before. The paralytic had sinned against God. Then along came Jesus, who under his own authority said, "Your sins are forgiven." Yes, we can forgive sins committed against us, but in no way can

> **What Do You Think?**
>
> *In this instance, why do you think Jesus said to the paralyzed man, "Your sins are forgiven" instead of "Stand up and walk"?*

> **What Do You Think?**
>
> *Do you agree that no one can forgive sins committed against God except God himself?*

anyone forgive sins committed against God except God himself. Yet that is what Jesus claimed to do.

It's no wonder the Jews reacted so violently when a carpenter from Nazareth made such a bold claim. This assertion that he could forgive sin was a startling exercise of a prerogative that belongs only to God.

Another situation in which Jesus claimed to be the Son of God was at his trial (see Mark 14:60-64). Those trial proceedings contain some of the clearest references to Jesus' claims of deity. "Then the high priest stood up before the others and asked Jesus, 'Well, aren't you going to answer these charges? What do you have to say for yourself?' Jesus made no reply. Then the high priest asked him, 'Are you the Messiah, the Son of the blessed God?' Jesus said, 'I am, and you will see me, the Son of Man, sitting at God's right hand in the place of power and coming back on the clouds of heaven' " (Mark 14:60-62).

> **We can forgive sins committed against us, but in no way can anyone forgive sins committed against God except God himself. Yet that is what Jesus claimed to do.**

At first Jesus wouldn't answer, so the high priest put him under oath. Because Jesus was under oath, he had to answer (and I'm so glad he did). He responded to the question, "Are you the Messiah, the Son of the blessed God?" by saying, "I am."

Jesus' reference to "the Son of Man" who would be "coming on the clouds of heaven," was an allusion to Daniel 7:13-14 (NASB):

I kept looking in the night visions,
And behold, with the clouds of heaven
One like a Son of Man was coming,
And He came up to the Ancient of Days
And was presented before Him.
And to Him was given dominion, Glory and
    a kingdom,
That all the peoples, nations, and men of every
    language
Might serve Him.
His dominion is an everlasting dominion
Which will not pass away;
And His kingdom is one
Which will not be destroyed.

Despite the common misperception, the term "Son of Man" was not a reference to the humanity of Jesus, but to his divinity. When Jesus referred to himself as the Son of Man he was referring to his divinity. In *Putting Jesus in His Place*, Rob Bowman and Ed Komoszewski explain how this applies to Daniel's vision:

> In Daniel's vision, the humanlike figure possesses all judgment authority and rules over an everlasting kingdom. The notion of frailty and dependence is absent. The description of the figure as coming with the clouds also identifies him as divine, since elsewhere in the Old Testament the imagery of coming on clouds is used exclusively for divine figures.[6]

Thus, in his allusion to Daniel 7:13, Jesus was claiming to be a divine, heavenly figure who would sit at God's right hand, exercising supreme authority over all people for eternity. No wonder the Jewish authorities were so upset—Jesus had committed blasphemy by claiming to be God! Clearly, Jesus had a divine self-consciousness.

An analysis of Christ's testimony shows that he claimed to be (1) the Son of the blessed God; (2) the One who would sit at the right hand of power; and (3) the Son of Man, who would come on the clouds of heaven. Each of these affirmations is distinctly messianic. The cumulative effect of all three is significant. The Sanhedrin, the Jewish court, caught all three points, and the high priest responded by tearing his garments and saying, "Why do we need other witnesses?" (Mark 14:63). They had finally heard it for themselves from Jesus' own mouth. He was convicted by his own words.

Sir Robert Anderson, who was once head of criminal investigation at Scotland Yard, points out:

> No confirmatory evidence is more convincing than that of hostile witnesses, and the fact that the Lord laid claim to Deity is incontestably established by the action of His enemies. We must remember that the Jews were not a tribe of ignorant savages, but a highly cultured and intensely religious people; and it was upon this very charge that, without a dissenting voice, His death was decreed by the Sanhedrin—their great national Council, composed of the most eminent of their religious leaders, including men of the type of Gamaliel, the great first century Jewish philosopher and his famous pupil, Saul of Tarsus.[7]

It is clear, then, that this is the testimony Jesus wanted to bear about himself. We also see that the Jews understood his reply was his claim to be God. At this point they faced two alternatives: that his assertions were outlandish blasphemy or that he was God. His judges saw the issue clearly—so clearly, in fact, that they crucified him and then taunted him because "he trusted God. . . . For he said, 'I am the Son of God' " (Matthew 27:43).

What Do You Think?
In some respects, doesn't the reaction of the Jewish leaders to Jesus' claims actually support those claims? If you had been a Jewish leader, what would you have done?

H. B. Swete, former Regius professor of divinity at Cambridge University, explains the significance of the high priest tearing his garment:

> The law forbade the High Priest to rend his garment in private troubles (Leviticus 10:6; 21:10), but when acting as a judge, he was required by custom to express in this way his horror of any blasphemy uttered in his presence. The relief of the embarrassed judge is manifest. If trustworthy evidence is not forthcoming, the necessity for it had now been superseded: the Prisoner had incriminated Himself.[8]

We begin to see that this was no ordinary trial. As lawyer Irwin Linton points out,

> Unique among criminal trials is this one in which not the actions but the identity of the

accused is the issue. The criminal charge laid against Christ, the confession or testimony or, rather, act in presence of the court, on which He was convicted, the interrogation by the Roman governor and the inscription and proclamation on His cross at the time of execution all are concerned with the one question of Christ's real identity and dignity. "What think ye of Christ? Whose son is he?"[9]

New York Supreme Court Justice William Jay Gaynor, in his address on the trial of Jesus, takes the position that blasphemy was the one charge made against him before the Sanhedrin. Referring to John 10:33, he says: "It is plain from each of the gospel narratives, that the alleged crime for which Jesus was tried and convicted was blasphemy: . . . Jesus had been claiming supernatural power, which in a human being was blasphemy."[10]

In most trials the accused are tried for what they are alleged to have done, but this was not the case in the trial of Jesus. He was tried for who he claimed to be.

In most trials the accused are tried for what they are alleged to have done, but this was not the case in the trial of Jesus. He was tried for who he *claimed to be*.

The trial of Jesus should be sufficient to demonstrate convincingly that he confessed to his divinity. His judges attest to that claim. But also, on the day of Christ's crucifixion, his enemies acknowledged that he claimed to be God come in the flesh.

The leading priests, the teachers of religious law, and the elders also mocked Jesus. "He saved others," they scoffed, "but he can't save himself! So he is the King of Israel, is he? Let him come down from the cross right now, and we will believe in him! He trusted God, so let God rescue him now if he wants him! For he said, 'I am the Son of God.'" MATTHEW 27:41-43

CHAPTER 3

Lord, Liar, or Lunatic?

IF YOU WERE TO GOOGLE THE NAME JESUS TODAY, YOU'D instantly get about 181 million hits. Search for Jesus at Amazon.com and you'll find 261,474 books about him. Given the smorgasbord of competing views, can we still have confidence in the historical Jesus? Many people want to regard Jesus not as God but as a good, moral man or as an exceptionally wise prophet who spoke many profound truths. Scholars often pass off that conclusion as the only acceptable one that people can reach by the intellectual process. Many people simply nod their heads in agreement and never trouble themselves to see the fallacy of such reasoning.

Jesus claimed to be God, and to him it was of fundamental importance that men and women believed him to be who he was. Either we believe him, or we don't. He didn't leave us any wiggle room for in-between, watered-down alternatives. One who claimed what Jesus claimed about himself couldn't be a good moral man or a prophet.

That option isn't open to us, and Jesus never intended it to be.

C. S. Lewis, former professor at Cambridge University and once an agnostic, understood this issue clearly. He writes:

> I am trying here to prevent anyone saying the really foolish thing that people often say about Him: 'I'm ready to accept Jesus as a great moral teacher, but I don't accept His claim to be God.' That is the one thing we must not say. A man who was merely a man and said the sort of things Jesus said would not be a great moral teacher. He would either be a lunatic—on a level with the man who says he is a poached egg— or else he would be the Devil of Hell. You must make your choice. Either this man was, and is, the Son of God: or else a madman or something worse.

Then Lewis adds:

> You can shut Him up for a fool, you can spit at Him and kill Him as a demon, or you can fall at His feet and call Him Lord and God. But let us not come up with any patronizing nonsense about his being a great human teacher. He has not left that open to us. He did not intend to.[1]

Cambridge University professor F. J. A. Hort, who spent twenty-eight years in a critical study of the New Testament text, writes:

> [Christ's] words were so completely parts and utterances of Himself, that they had no meaning

as abstract statements of truth uttered by Him as a Divine oracle or prophet. Take away Himself as the primary (though not the ultimate) subject of every statement and they all fall to pieces.[2]

In the words of Kenneth Scott Latourette, historian of Christianity at Yale University:

It is not his teachings which make Jesus so remarkable, although these would be enough to give him distinction. It is a combination of the teachings with the man himself. The two cannot be separated.

Latourette concludes,

It must be obvious to any thoughtful reader of the Gospel records that Jesus regarded himself and his message as inseparable. He was a great teacher, but he was more. His teachings about the kingdom of God, about human conduct, and about God were important, but they could not be divorced from him without, from his standpoint, being vitiated.[3]

Jesus claimed to be God. His claim must be either true or false, and everyone should give it the same kind of consideration he expected of his disciples when he put the question to them: "Who do you say I am?" (Matthew 16:15). There are several alternatives.

First, consider that his claim to be God was false. If it were false, then we have only two alternatives. He either knew it was false, or he didn't know it was false. We will consider each possibility separately and examine the evidence for it.

Was Jesus a Liar?

If, when Jesus made his claims, he knew that he was not God, then he was lying and deliberately deceiving his followers. But if he was a liar, then he was also a hypocrite because he taught others to be honest whatever the cost. Worse than that, if he was lying, he was a demon because he told others to trust him for their eternal destiny. If he couldn't back up his claims and knew it, then he was unspeakably evil for deceiving his followers with such a false hope. Last, he would also be a fool because his claims to being God led to his crucifixion—claims he could have backed away from to save himself even at the last minute.

> "Let us not come up with any patronizing nonsense about [Jesus] being a great human teacher. He has not left that open to us. He did not intend to."
> –C.S. Lewis

What Do You Think?

Why can't you say that Jesus was just a good moral teacher? Can you think of any specific "good morals" that he taught his followers that still make sense today?

It amazes me to hear so many people say that Jesus was simply a good moral teacher. Let's be realistic. How could he be a great moral teacher and knowingly mislead people at the most important point of his teaching—his own identity?

To conclude that Jesus was a deliberate liar doesn't coincide with what we know either of him or of the results of his life and teachings. Wherever Jesus has been proclaimed, we see lives change for the good, nations change for the better, thieves become honest, alcoholics become sober, hateful individuals become channels of love, unjust persons embrace justice.

William Lecky, one of Great Britain's most noted historians and a fierce opponent of organized Christianity, saw the effect of true Christianity on the world. He writes:

> It was reserved for Christianity to present to the world an ideal which through all the changes of eighteen centuries has inspired the hearts of men with an impassioned love; has shown itself capable of acting on all ages, nations, temperaments, and conditions; has been not only the highest pattern of virtue, but the strongest incentive to its practice. . . . The simple record of these three short years of active life has done more to regenerate and soften mankind than all the disquisitions of philosophers and all the exhortations of moralists.[4]

Historian Philip Schaff says:

> This testimony [that Jesus was God], if not true, must be downright blasphemy or madness. . . . Self-deception in a matter so momentous, and with an intellect in all respects so clear and so sound, is equally out of the question. How could he be an enthusiast or a madman who never lost the even balance of his mind, who sailed serenely over all the troubles and persecutions, as the sun above the clouds, who always returned the wisest answer to tempting questions, who calmly and deliberately predicted his death on the cross, his resurrection on the third day, the outpouring of the Holy Spirit,

the founding of his Church, the destruction of
Jerusalem—predictions which have been literally
fulfilled? A character so original, so complete, so
uniformly consistent, so perfect, so human and set
so high above all human greatness, can be neither
a fraud nor a fiction. The poet, as has been well
said, would in this case be greater than the hero.
It would take more than a Jesus to invent a Jesus.[5]

Elsewhere Schaff gives convincing argument against
Christ being a liar:

How in the name of logic, common sense, and
experience, could an imposter—that is a deceitful,
selfish, depraved man—have invented, and
consistently maintained from the beginning to
end, the purest and noblest character known in
history with the most perfect air of truth and
reality? How could he have conceived and carried
out a plan of unparalleled beneficence, moral
magnitude, and sublimity, and sacrificed his own
life for it, in the face of the strongest prejudices
of his people and age?[6]

If Jesus wanted to get people to follow him and believe
in him as God, why did he go to the Jewish nation? Why
go as a common carpenter in an undistinguished village
in a country so small in size and population? Why go to
a country that so thoroughly adhered to the concept of
one God? Why didn't he go to Egypt, or even to Greece,
where they already believed in various gods and various
manifestations of them?

Someone who lived as Jesus lived, taught as Jesus taught, and died as Jesus died could not have been a liar. Let's look at other alternatives.

Was Jesus a Lunatic?

If we find it inconceivable that Jesus was a liar, then couldn't he actually have mistakenly thought himself to be God? After all, it's possible to be both sincere and wrong. But we must remember that for someone to mistakenly think himself God, especially in the context of a fiercely monotheistic culture, and then to tell others that their eternal destiny depended on believing in him, is no small flight of fancy but the delusions and ravings of an outright lunatic. Is it possible that Jesus Christ was deranged?

> **What Do You Think?**
> *Why do you think Jesus took his message to the Jewish nation? Do you think there was any advantage to him being a carpenter before his ministry began?*

Today we would treat someone who believes himself to be God the same way we would treat someone who believes he is Napoleon. We would see him as deluded and self-deceived. We would lock him up so he wouldn't hurt himself or anyone else. Yet in Jesus we don't observe the abnormalities and imbalance that go along with such derangement. If he was insane, his poise and composure was nothing short of amazing.

Eminent psychiatric pioneers Arthur Noyes and Lawrence Kolb, in their *Modern Clinical Psychiatry* text, describe the schizophrenic as a person who is more autistic than realistic. The schizophrenic desires to escape from the world of reality. Let's face it—for a mere man to claim to be God would certainly be a retreat from reality.

What Do You Think?

Is there anything you detect in Jesus' behavior (other than his claim to divinity) that would suggest he was deranged? If you had lived in his day, would you have wanted to hear him?

In light of other things we know about Jesus, it's hard to imagine that he was mentally disturbed. Here is a man who spoke some of the most profound words ever recorded. His instructions have liberated many people in mental bondage. Clark H. Pinnock, professor emeritus of systematic theology at McMaster Divinity College, asks: "Was he deluded about his greatness, a paranoid, an unintentional deceiver, a schizophrenic? Again, the skill and depth of his teaching support the case only for his total mental soundness. If only we were as sane as he!"[7] A student at a California university told me that his psychology professor had said in class that "all he has to do is pick up the Bible and read portions of Christ's teaching to many of his patients. That's all the counseling they need."

Psychologist Gary R. Collins explains that Jesus

> was loving but didn't let his compassion
> immobilize him; he didn't have a bloated ego,
> even though he was often surrounded by adoring
> crowds; he maintained balance despite an often
> demanding lifestyle; he always knew what he was
> doing and where he was going; he cared deeply
> about people, including women and children, who

weren't seen as important back then; he was able to accept people while not merely winking at their sin; he responded to individuals based on where they were at and what they uniquely needed. All in all, I just don't see signs that Jesus was suffering from any known mental illness. . . . He was much healthier than anyone else I know—including me![8]

Psychiatrist J. T. Fisher felt that Jesus' teachings were profound. He states:

If you were to take the sum total of all authoritative articles ever written by the most qualified of psychologists and psychiatrists on the subject of mental hygiene—if you were to combine them and refine them and cleave out the excess verbiage—if you were to take the whole of the meat and none of the parsley, and if you were to have these unadulterated bits of pure scientific knowledge concisely expressed by the most capable of living poets, you would have an awkward and incomplete summation of the Sermon on the Mount. And it would suffer immeasurably through comparison. For nearly two thousand years the Christian world has been holding in its hands the complete answer to its restless and fruitless yearnings. Here . . . rests the blueprint for successful human life with optimism, mental health, and contentment.[9]

For a mere man to claim to be God would certainly be a retreat from reality.

C. S. Lewis writes:

> The historical difficulty of giving for the life, sayings and influence of Jesus any explanation that is not harder than the Christian explanation is very great. The discrepancy between the depth and sanity . . . of His moral teaching and the rampant megalomania which must lie behind His theological teaching unless He is indeed God has never been satisfactorily explained. Hence the non-Christian hypotheses succeed one another with the restless fertility of bewilderment.[10]

Philip Schaff reasons:

> Is such an intellect—clear as the sky, bracing as the mountain air, sharp and penetrating as a sword, thoroughly healthy and vigorous, always ready and always self-possessed—liable to a radical and most serious delusion concerning his own character and mission? Preposterous imagination![11]

Was Jesus Lord?

I cannot personally conclude that Jesus was a liar or a lunatic. The only other alternative is that he was—and is—the Christ, the Son of God, as he claimed. But in spite of the logic and evidence, many people cannot seem to bring themselves to this conclusion.

In *The Da Vinci Code* Dan Brown claims, "By officially endorsing Jesus as the Son of God, Constantine turned Jesus into a deity who existed beyond the scope of the human world, an entity whose power was unchallengeable."[12] Novelist Brown wants people to believe the idea that Christ's deity was invented at the Council of Nicea.

Although discussed prominently in popular culture, the "fact" has been rejected by well over 99.9 percent of biblical scholars who study documented history. Here's why.

What Do You Think?

Why do you think so many psychologists see Jesus as a model for health? Why was he so content?

The New Testament itself provides the earliest evidence for the belief that Jesus is divine (See chapter two). Since these documents were composed in the first century just decades after the events surrounding Jesus, they predate the Council of Nicea by more than two centuries. While they were written by different people for a variety of purposes, one unmistakable theme they share is that Christ is God.

The ante-Nicene fathers provide additional support that Jesus was considered divine long before the council of Nicea. The ante-Nicene fathers were early Christian thinkers who lived after the close of the New Testament period (c. 100), yet before the council of Nicea (325). The ante-Nicene fathers included men such as Justin Martyr, Ignatius, and Irenaeus. There is no doubt that they understood Jesus to be divine. Consider some quotes from their ancient works:

> Ignatius of Antioch (AD 110): "God incarnate . . . God Himself appearing in the form of man."[13]

> Justin Martyr (AD 100–165): ". . . being the First-begotten Word of God, is even God."[14]

Irenaeus (AD 177): ". . . the Father is God and the Son is God; for He who is born of God is God."[15]

Melito of Sardis (circa AD 177): "He was man, yet He is God."

Probably the most convincing evidence that Jesus was considered divine before Nicea comes from non-Christian writers. The Greek satirist Lucian of Samosata (c. AD 170), the Roman philosopher Celsus (c. 177), and the Roman governor Pliny the Younger (c. 112) make it clear that early Christians understood Jesus as divine. Pliny persecuted Christians because of their belief that Jesus was divine. Pliny acknowledged: "They had met regularly before dawn on a fixed day to chant verses alternately among themselves in honour of Christ as if to a god."[16]

Given these facts, in addition to many more, the authors of *Reinventing Jesus* conclude: "To suggest that Constantine had the ability—or even the inclination—to manipulate the council into believing what it did not already embrace is, at best, a silly notion."[17] The evidence is clear: Jesus was believed to be divine long before the council of Nicea.

I cannot personally conclude that Jesus was a liar or a lunatic. The only other alternative is that he was—and is—the Christ, the Son of God.

When I discuss the material in this chapter with most Jewish or Muslim people, their response is quite interesting. I share with them the claims Jesus made about himself and then put to them the options: Was he contained in the trilemma (liar, lunatic, or Lord)? When I ask if they believe Jesus was a liar, they give me a sharp "No!" Then I ask, "Do you believe he was a lunatic?" Their reply is, "Of course not." "Do you believe he is God?" Before I can get a word in edgewise, I hear a resounding "Absolutely not!" Yet one has no more choices.

What Do You Think?
If the evidence for the deity of Jesus is so clear, why do you think so many people still reject it?

The issue with these three alternatives is not which is possible, for obviously all three are possible. Rather, the question is, "Which is most probable?" You cannot put him on the shelf merely as a great moral teacher or a prophet. That is not a valid option. He is either a liar, a lunatic, or Lord and God. You must make a choice. Your decision about Jesus must be more than an idle intellectual exercise. As the apostle John wrote, "These are written so that you may continue to believe that Jesus is the Messiah, the Son of God, and"—more important—"that by believing in him you will have life by the power of his name" (John 20:31).

The evidence is clearly in favor of Jesus as Lord.

CHAPTER 4

What about Science?

MANY PEOPLE TRY TO PUT OFF PERSONAL COMMITMENT TO Christ on the assumption that if you cannot prove something scientifically, it is therefore not true. Since one cannot scientifically prove the deity of Jesus or his resurrection, then twenty-first-century sophisticates should know better than to accept him as Savior.

Often in a philosophy or history class someone confronts me with the challenge, "Can you prove it scientifically?" I usually say, "Well, no, I'm not a scientist." Then I hear the class chuckling and several voices saying things like, "Then don't talk to me about it," or "See, you must take it all by faith" (meaning blind faith).

Once on a flight to Boston I was talking with the passenger next to me about why I personally believe Christ is who he claimed to be. The pilot, making his public-relations rounds and greeting the passengers, overheard part of our conversation. "You have a problem with your belief," he said.

"What is that?" I asked.

"You can't prove it scientifically," he replied.

I am amazed at the inconsistency to which modern thinking has descended. This pilot is like so many people in this century who hold the opinion that if you can't prove a thing scientifically, it can't be true. We all accept as true many facts that cannot be verified by scientific methods. We cannot scientifically prove anything about any person or event in history, but that doesn't mean that proof is impossible. We need to understand the difference between scientific proof and what I call legal-historical proof. Let me explain.

What Do You Think?
Besides historical facts, are there any other things we know to be true that are not provable scientifically? If so, what are they?

Scientific proof is based on showing that something is a fact by repeating the event in the presence of the person questioning the fact. It is done in a controlled environment where observations can be made, data drawn, and hypotheses empirically verified.

Many people hold the opinion that if you can't prove a thing scientifically, it can't be true.

The "scientific method, however it is defined, is related to measurement of phenomena and experimentation or repeated observation."[1] Dr. James B. Conant, former president of Harvard, writes:

> Science is an interconnected series of concepts and conceptual schemes that have developed

as a result of experimentation and observation, and are fruitful of further experimentation and observations.[2]

Testing the truth of a hypothesis by the use of controlled experiments is one of the key techniques of the modern scientific method. For example, someone claims that Ivory soap doesn't float. I claim it does float, so to prove my point, I take the doubter to the kitchen, put eight inches of water in the sink at 82.7 degrees, and drop in the soap. *Plunk!* We make observations, we draw data, and we verify my hypothesis empirically: Ivory soap floats.

If the scientific method were the only method we had for proving facts, you couldn't prove that you watched television last night or that you had lunch today. There's no way you could repeat those events in a controlled situation.

The other method of proof, the *legal-historical proof*, is based on showing that something is a fact beyond a reasonable doubt. In other words, we reach a verdict on the weight of the evidence and have no rational basis for doubting the decision. Legal-historical proof depends on three kinds of testimony: oral testimony, written testimony, and exhibits (such as a gun, a bullet, or a notebook). Using the legal-historical method to determine the facts, you could prove beyond a reasonable doubt that you went to lunch today. Your friends

If the scientific method were the only method we had for proving facts, you couldn't prove that you had lunch today. There's no way you could repeat that event in a controlled situation.

saw you there, the waiter remembers seeing you, and you have the restaurant receipt.

The scientific method can be used to prove only repeatable things. It isn't adequate for proving or disproving questions about persons or events in history. The scientific method isn't appropriate for answering such questions as: Did George Washington live? Was Martin Luther King Jr. a civil rights leader? Who was Jesus of Nazareth? Does Barry Bonds hold major league baseball's one-season home run record? Was Jesus Christ raised from the dead? These questions are outside the realm of scientific proof, and we must place them in the realm of legal-historical proof. In other words, the scientific method—which is based on observation, information gathering, hypothesizing, deduction, and experimental verification to find and explain empirical regularities in nature—cannot uncover the final answers to such questions as: Can you prove the Resurrection? Is science at war with religion? Has science somehow disproved the existence of God? In the next chapter my son, Sean, examines the claims of the "New Atheists"— who believe that very thing.

What Do You Think?

What are the advantages of using the scientific method to "prove" something? What are the disadvantages? What are the advantages of using the legal-historical method of proof? Do you find yourself using one method over another more frequently?

CHAPTER 5

The Challenge of the New Atheism

As I (Sean) sat down at the local coffee house to sip my iced vanilla latte, I looked across the room and noticed a young woman reading a book with a very provocative title. The silver letters jumped out from the bright yellow background: *God Is Not Great: How Religion Poisons Everything*, by Christopher Hitchens. Intrigued by the bold title, I decided to ask her what the book was about. She proceeded to give me an enthusiastic, lengthy lecture about how religion has been the greatest force of evil in world history, how science has disproved any basis for rational faith, and how people can be good without God.

Was this young woman right? Is religion the bane of human existence? Has science somehow disproved God? Would the world be better if we all embraced atheism?

Atheism is certainly not new. About 1,000 years before the coming of Christ, King David described a person who says in his heart, "There is no God" (Psalm 14:1). There have always been people who deny the existence of God, and there probably always will be. While atheists have often been vocal about their beliefs, their pop-cultural influence has been minimal. Until now.

Recently a group of articulate, enthusiastic, and militant atheists have exploded onto the public scene. The audience they have commandeered is unprecedented in the history of atheism. In just over a year, three of their books hit the shelves. Sam Harris began the assault with the release of *Letter to a Christian Nation* (2006), followed by Richard Dawkins's *The God Delusion* (2006), and finally Christopher Hitchens's *God Is Not Great* (2007). All three books quickly experienced explosive sales, spending months—not weeks—on multiple best seller lists. *God Is Not Great*, for example, debuted at number 1 on the *New York Times* hardcover nonfiction best seller list within a month of its release. Nearly 300,000 copies were in print by its seventh week.

The influence of these so-called New Atheists has gone far beyond the publishing world. They have written ten articles, spoken on college campuses, participated in debates, been interviewed on radio and TV, and posted countless videos on YouTube. They have confused seekers and rocked the faith of many believers. Recent polls indicate that an increasing number of Americans identify themselves as atheists and agnostics. The goal of the New Atheists is simple: to eradicate any rational grounds for religious belief and to persuade theists to walk away from their faith. Are they on to something new? Have they

What Do You Think?

Why do you think the New Atheists have recently commanded such a significant following?

uncovered some fresh evidence that disproves God? What makes the new atheism *new*?

Same Ol', Same Ol'

Renowned British journalist Malcolm Muggeridge once said that all news is nothing more than new people experiencing old things. Things may *seem* new, but that hardly means they really *are* new. When it comes to the New Atheism, there are no fresh discoveries in science, philosophy, or history that undermine Christianity. Most arguments of the New Atheists are recycled from older atheists such as Friedrich Nietzsche, Sigmund Freud, Karl Marx, and Bertrand Russell. Still, there are a few characteristics that make the New Atheists unique.

> **Many older atheists mourned the death of God. The New Atheists actually celebrate the death of God.**

First, the New Atheism is less costly. Atheists of the past were well aware of the consequences of denying God. They realized that without God we inhabit a cold, dark, pointless universe. Many older atheists mourned the death of God because they realized it undermined the foundations of Western culture. Existentialist Albert Camus admitted that the death of God meant the loss of purpose, joy, and everything that makes life worth living.

By contrast, the New Atheists actually celebrate the death of God. They think life can continue as normal (and even improve) if we simply abolish religion. Such "soft" atheism, says Professor John Haught of Georgetown University, fails to take atheism seriously:

The new soft-core atheists assume that, by dint of Darwinism, we can just drop God like Santa Claus without having to witness the complete collapse of Western culture—including our sense of what is rational and moral. At least the hard-core atheists understood that if we are truly sincere in our atheism the whole web of meanings and values that had clustered around the idea of God in Western culture has to go down the drain along with its organizing center.[1]

Second, in contrast to older forms of atheism, the New Atheists have no tolerance for religious faith. They believe that not only is religion man-made, but that it poisons everything and therefore needs to be eliminated. In *Letter to a Christian Nation*, Sam Harris says that "the respect [the Religious Right] demands for their own religious beliefs gives shelter to extremists of all faiths."[2] While Harris recognizes that liberals and moderates do not fly planes into buildings, he believes their tolerance lends support to such extremism. Therefore, it needs to be eradicated. If the New Atheists get their way, freedom of religion will be a relic of the past.

Third, the New Atheists reserve their most venomous attacks for Christianity. While they do criticize Buddhism, Islam, Mormonism, and other religions, their target is clearly the biblical God. Richard Dawkins acknowledges, "Unless otherwise stated, I shall have Christianity mostly in mind."[3]

If you've read any of the New Atheists, it's important to keep the words of King Solomon in mind: "The first to speak in court sounds right—until the cross-examination begins" (Proverbs 18:17). In other words, when only one side of a case is heard, the evidence often seems convincing. Yet when the whole story is in, the initial case often crumbles. The New Atheists are convincing—until the other side is heard. Here is the other side.

Is Atheism More Reasonable?

The New Atheists firmly believe that atheism holds the rational higher ground. According to Hitchens, religion is based upon "faith alone," whereas atheism requires no faith commitment since it relies primarily upon the empirical evidence of science.[4]

We will explore the question of whether atheism or theism best accounts for the scientific data, but first we need to consider a more basic question: why does the natural world make any sense to begin with? Einstein once remarked that the most incomprehensible thing about the world is that it is comprehensible.

Einstein understood a basic truth about science, namely, that it relies upon certain philosophical assumptions about the natural world. These assumptions include the existence of a real external world that is orderly and knowable, and the trustworthiness of our minds to grasp that world. Science cannot proceed apart from these assumptions.

> **Einstein once remarked that the most incomprehensible thing about the world is that it is comprehensible.**

But this raises a particularly thorny dilemma for the atheist: If the mind developed through the blind, material process of Darwinian evolution, then why should we trust it at all? Why should we believe that the human brain—which was the outcome of an accidental process—actually puts us in touch with reality? Science cannot be used as an answer to this question, because science itself relies upon these very assumptions.

Even Charles Darwin was aware of this problem: "The horrid doubt always arises whether the convictions of man's mind, which has been developed from the mind of lower animals, are of any value or at all trustworthy. Would anyone trust the conviction of a monkey's mind, if there are any convictions in such a mind?"[5] The New Atheists place enormous trust in their own powers of reason, but their atheistic worldview undermines any basis for such confidence. In fact, if Darwinian evolution is true, we should distrust our cognitive faculties since they are the result of an unguided, irrational process.

If Darwinian evolution is true, we should distrust our cognitive faculties since they are the result of an unguided, irrational process.

Templeton Prize–winning physicist Paul Davies said, "Science is based on the assumption that the universe is thoroughly rational and logical at every level. Atheists claim that the laws [of nature] exist reasonlessly and that the universe is ultimately absurd. As a scientist, I find this hard to accept. There must be an unchanging rational ground in which the logical, orderly nature of the universe is rooted."[6]

Atheism provides no such rational ground. In fact, atheism undercuts it. Theism, however, provides such a foundation. It's not simply that the rationality of the universe fits better with theism. The level of connection goes deeper. A rational universe is what we would expect if God exists.

Is Science at War with Religion?

Science has been at war with religion for centuries. At least that's what the New Atheists want you to think. Although widely believed, it is a myth that religion has been impeding the growth of science.[7] It's actually the Christian worldview—with its insistence on the orderliness of the universe, its emphasis on human reason, and its teaching that God is glorified in our understanding of his creation—that laid the foundation for the modern scientific revolution.

What Do You Think?

Why would we expect the universe to be rational if God exists? How, exactly, does atheism undercut the basis of rationality?

Most early scientists were compelled to study the natural world because of their Christian worldview. In *Science and the Modern World*, British mathematician and philosopher Alfred North Whitehead concludes that modern science developed primarily from "the medieval insistence on the rationality of God."[8]

Modern science did not develop in a vacuum, but from forces largely propelled by Christianity. Not surprisingly, most early scientists were theists, including pioneers such as Francis Bacon (1561–1626), Johannes Kepler (1571–1630), Blaise Pascal (1623–62), Robert Boyle (1627–91), Isaac Newton (1642–1727), and Louis Pasteur (1822–95). For many of them, belief in God was the prime motivation for their investigation of the natural world. Bacon believed the natural world was full of mysteries God intended for us to explore. Kepler described his motivation for science: "The chief aim of all investigations of the external world should be to discover the rational order and harmony which has been imposed on it by God, and which he revealed to us in the language of mathematics."[9]

Hitchens discounts the religious convictions of these scientific pioneers, arguing that there was no other live alternative for an intellectual of the time.[10] But this puts Hitchens in a curious position. If religious believers get no credit for the positive contributions they made to society (e.g., shaping modern science) because "everyone was religious," then how can religious believers be blamed for the atrocities committed in the name of God? This is a clear double standard. The New Atheists want to deny religious believers any credit, yet give them all the blame. To make the case that "religion poisons everything," Hitchens has to overlook all evidence to the contrary. And he is happy to do so.

Is Atheism More Scientific?

The confidence of the New Atheists stems from one central fact: they believe science is on their side. Sam Harris says, "Belief in the biblical God finds no support in our growing scientific understanding of the world."[11] And according to Hitchens, the more science develops, the less room there is for God.[12] But is this the whole story? While the New Atheists would like us to believe that God can only be inferred from the "gaps" in our scientific knowledge, in reality, the scientific evidence for design has exploded in recent years.[13] In fact, one of the most influential atheists of the past five decades—Antony Flew—recently changed his mind about God for this very reason.

While other atheists may have been more recognizable, Flew's impact was unparalleled. He delivered his famous lecture, "Theology and Falsification," at the Socratic Club at Oxford, then chaired by C. S. Lewis. It eventually became the most widely reprinted philosophical article for five decades. His many books and lectures set the agenda for modern atheism.

Then in 2004, Flew made a shocking announcement: God must exist. Flew now believes that the best explanation for the world is some sort of deity. Why did he change his mind? "The short answer," writes Flew, "is the world picture, as I see it, that has emerged from modern science."[14] The New Atheists are free to proclaim that science is on their side, but the evidence shows the contrary. Consider two recent scientific puzzles that remain unexplained by naturalistic science, but point strongly toward God.

> **What Do You Think?**
> *In your view, is the scientific evidence in favor of God's existence, against God's existence, or neutral? On what do you base your opinion?*

The mystery of the origin of life

One of the most perplexing scientific problems today is the origin of life. The scientific community is unanimous that this is an unsolved mystery. Harvard chemist George Whitesides once remarked that the question of life's origin is one of the big scientific questions that has yet to be solved.[15] Even Sam Harris admits that the origin of life is still a mystery.[16]

The problem of the origin of life is fundamentally a problem of information.

With the discovery of the structure of DNA in 1953, scientists first understood that the organization and development of living creatures is orchestrated by genetic information. This is why, in a widely cited speech, Nobel laureate David Baltimore referred to modern biology as "a science of information."

How much information is found in living things? According to Richard Dawkins, the information in the cell nucleus of a tiny amoeba is greater than an entire set of the *Encyclopaedia Britannica*.[17] Human DNA contains vastly more. Yet DNA does more than just store information. In combination with other cellular systems, it also processes information much like a computer. Hence Bill Gates likens DNA to a computer program, though far more advanced than any software humans have invented.[18]

What Do You Think?

Is luck a credible deduction for the origin of life? Apart from God, can you think of any other reasonable explanation?

Atheists willingly confess that they have no clue how life first emerged. Dawkins recognizes the staggering improbability of the origin of life, but then concludes with an incredible solution: luck. Yes, luck.[19] Is this really the most reasonable explanation? Can information emerge from an unguided, irrational, material process?

The informational content of DNA was one of the primary reasons former atheist Antony Flew changed his mind about God. He concluded: "The only satisfactory explanation for the origin of such 'end-directed, self-replicating' life as we see on earth is an infinitely intelligent Mind."[20] If a message with the complexity of the *Encyclopaedia Britannica* were to arrive from outer space, it would undoubtedly be accepted as proof of extraterrestrial intelligence. The most reasonable explanation for human

DNA—which contains immensely more information than the *Encyclopaedia Britannica*—is a Divine Mind.

Fine-tuning the universe

Imagine you are trekking through the mountains and come across an abandoned cabin. As you approach the cabin, you notice something very strange. Inside, the refrigerator is filled with your favorite food, the temperature is set just as you like it, your favorite song is playing in the background, and all your favorite books, magazines, and DVDs are sitting on the table. What would you conclude? Since chance would be out of the question, you would likely conclude that someone was expecting your arrival.

In recent decades, scientists have begun to realize that this scenario mirrors the universe as a whole. The universe seems to have been crafted uniquely with us in mind. "As we look out into the universe and identify the many accidents of physics and astronomy that have worked to our benefit," says physicist Freeman J. Dyson, "it almost seems as if the universe must in some sense have known that we were coming."[21] This is why British astronomer Fred Hoyle remarked, "A commonsense interpretation of the facts suggests that a super intellect has monkeyed with physics, as well as chemistry and biology, and that there are no blind forces worth speaking about in nature."[22] Physicists agree that life is balanced on a razor's edge.

> "The only satisfactory explanation for the origin of such 'end-directed, self-replicating' life as we see on earth is an infinitely intelligent Mind."
> –Antony Flew, former leading atheist

Consider a couple of examples. First, if the law of gravity varied just slightly, the universe would not be habitable for life. In relation to the other forces in nature, gravity must be fine-tuned to one part in 10^{40} (that's one part in 10,000,000,000,000,000,000,000,000,000,000,000,000,000).[23] Second, Cambridge physicist Stephen Hawking observed that, "If the rate of expansion one second after the Big Bang had been smaller by even one part in a hundred thousand million million, the universe would have recollapsed before it even reached its present size."[24]

The universe seems to have been crafted uniquely with humans in mind.

There are actually nineteen such universal constants that must each be perfectly fine-tuned.[25] Clearly, the odds against us being here are vanishingly small. In fact, Oxford physicist Roger Penrose concluded that if we jointly considered all the laws of nature that must be fine-tuned, we would be unable to write down such an enormous number, since the necessary digits would be greater than the number of elementary particles in the universe.[26]

The evidence for design is so compelling that Paul Davies, a renowned physicist at Arizona State University, has concluded that the bio-friendly nature of our universe looks like a "fix." He put it this way: "The cliché that 'life is balanced on a knife-edge' is a staggering understatement in this case: no knife in the universe could have an edge that fine."[27] No scientific explanation for the universe, says Davies, can be complete without accounting for this overwhelming appearance of design. Some try to explain away the fine-tuning by positing the existence of multiple universes, but the empirical evidence for them is nonexistent. The most economical and reliable explanation for why the universe is so precisely fine-tuned is because a Creator—God—made it that way.

Is Atheism More Moral?

The New Atheists unmercifully attack the evils of religion and the character of the biblical God. Morality can exist independently of God, they loudly proclaim. According to Dawkins, "We do not need God in order to be good—or evil."[28] The New Atheists enthusiastically denounce religion as evil while praising science as good. But this raises an awkward dilemma for the atheist: if there is no God, where do moral obligations come from in the first place? If "there is nothing beyond the natural, physical world,"[29] as Dawkins proclaims, then what does it mean to say that evil exists? Since moral values do not have physical properties such as height, width, and weight, how can we say they are real?

The awkward fact for atheism is that it is notoriously difficult to define evil without some transcendent moral standard of good. Evil has traditionally been understood as the perversion of good. Just as crookedness implies a standard of straight, evil implies a standard of good. C. S. Lewis famously said that a bent stick only makes sense in light of the concept of straight. Similarly, there can only be evil if there is first good. But if there is no God (as the New

> **What Do You Think?**
> *Russian novelist Fyodor Dostoyevsky famously said that without God all is permissible. What do you think he meant? Can there be a moral standard without God?*

Atheists proclaim), then what is good? Even the late atheist J. L. Mackie recognized that objective morals were unlikely to arise apart from an all-powerful God.

The existence of objective moral values is a strong reason for believing in God. Consider this simple argument:

1. If objective moral values exist, God must exist.
2. Objective moral values exist.
3. Therefore, God must exist.

We know objective moral values exist. We don't need to be persuaded that, for example, torturing babies for fun is wrong. All reasonable people know this. Therefore, since moral values do exist, then God must as well.

In his public debates, Christopher Hitchens regularly challenges his opponents to give a single example of a moral action that atheists cannot do. Of course, there are none. Many atheists are kind, charitable, and hard-working people. But Hitchens's challenge misses the larger point: how can atheism itself make sense of moral obligations in the first place? If there is no God, how do we ground good and evil? Atheism is silent on this issue. Thus, ironically, one of the most common objections to God ends up being one of the best reasons to believe in him.

It is notoriously difficult to define evil without some transcendent moral standard of good.

Is Christianity a Curse?

The old atheists believed religion was false. The New Atheists believe it is not only false, but evil. Sam Harris calls religion, "the most potent source of human conflict, past and present."[30] The New Atheists repeatedly point to the maltreatment of Galileo, the atrocities of the Crusades, the Inquisition, and the Salem witch trials in past history, as well as the sexual abuse of children by Catholic priests in today's world as evidence of the cruelty of Christianity.

People have undoubtedly done horrific things in the name of Christ. But why should Christianity take the blame when it is people who are doing the opposite of what Jesus taught? Did Jesus favor burning witches? Did Jesus encourage his followers to torture heretics? Of course not. In fact, Jesus taught the exact opposite. He said to love your enemies (Matthew 5:44), to reach out to those whom society considers untouchable (Matthew 8:3), and to lay down your life for others (John 15:13). If people really did live like Jesus, violence would likely be a thing of the past.

What Do You Think?

If people lived according to the teachings of Jesus, what would the world really be like? Should Christianity bear the blame when people do the opposite of what Jesus teaches?

In *What's So Great about Christianity*, Dinesh D'Souza demonstrates that the New Atheists grossly exaggerate the crimes committed in the name of religion while rationalizing the vastly greater crimes committed in the name of atheism. For example, Sam Harris estimates the number of people who were killed in the Salem witch trials to be 100,000. What is the real number? Hundreds? thousands? tens of thousands? Actually, it's fewer than twenty-five.[31] But how does atheism fare?

It's important to keep in mind that the issue is not whether individual atheists can be good people. Of course they can (and many are). The key question is whether atheism, when it is adopted as the prevailing philosophy for a particular culture, is good or bad. When this question is the standard, it becomes clear that no other fundamental worldview has caused as much misery and bloodshed as atheism. Specifically, the number of people slaughtered by twentieth-century atheistic regimes, such as communist China, communist Russia, and Nazi Germany is more than one hundred million people.[32] There is no close second place. David Berlinski, a secular Jew who received his PhD from Princeton University, believes that one of the main reasons for such atrocities is the absence of ultimate accountability: "What Hitler did not believe and what Stalin did not believe and what Mao did not believe and what the SS did not believe and what the Gestapo did not believe . . . was that God was watching what they were doing."[33]

While Christians have certainly done some bad things, the legacy of Christianity has been overwhelmingly positive.

While Christians have certainly done some bad things, the legacy of Christianity has been overwhelmingly positive. Christians built the first hospitals, started the Red Cross, led the movement to end slavery, invented the university, and pioneered modern science. When we trace the movements that have led to the most profound liberation for humanity, we find the gospel at the heart of almost all of them.

Conclusion

In the final analysis, the only thing really new about the New Atheists is their attitude. Despite the flaming rhetoric, there are no recent findings in science, history, or philosophy that undermine theism in general or Christianity in particular. In fact, precisely the opposite is the case. The more we descend into the interworkings of the cell or ascend to the depths of the universe, the more we can see the fingerprint of God.

Roughly 3,000 years ago the psalmist said it best: "The heavens proclaim the glory of God. The skies display his craftsmanship. Day after day they continue to speak; night after night they make him known" (Psalm 19:1-2). As this psalm so clearly enunciates, God can be known through his creation. Yet as this book demonstrates, he has made himself known specifically through the person of Jesus Christ, who is more than a carpenter. This is not something we accept by blind faith, but through compelling evidence.

Can we prove that Jesus is the Son of God? Only the legal-historical method will work to prove such a question. Then the primary question becomes this: can we trust the reliability of the testimonies and evidences (i.e., the New Testament)?

One thing about the Christian faith that has especially appealed to me (Josh) is that it is not a blind, ignorant belief but rather one based on solid intelligence. Every time we read that a Bible character was asked to exercise faith, we see that it's an intelligent faith. Jesus said, "You will know the truth" (John 8:32), not ignore it. Christ was asked, "Which is the most important commandment?" Jesus replied, "You must love

One thing about the Christian faith that has appealed to me is that it is not a blind, ignorant belief but rather one based on solid intelligence.

the LORD your God with all your heart, all your soul, and *all your mind*" (Matthew 22:36-37, emphasis mine). The problem with many people is that they seem to love God only with their hearts. The truth about Christ never gets to their minds. We've been given minds enabled by the Holy Spirit to know God, as well as hearts to love him and wills to choose him. We need to function in all three areas to have a full relationship with God and to glorify him. I don't know how it is with you, but my heart can't

What Do You Think?

Is the idea of an intelligent faith new to you? If faith is "not a blind, ignorant belief but rather one based on solid intelligence," then what would be a fitting definition of faith?

rejoice in what my mind has rejected. My heart and mind were created to work in harmony together. Never has anyone been called on to commit intellectual suicide by trusting Christ as Savior and Lord.

In the next four chapters we will take a look at the evidence for the reliability of the written documents and for the credibility of the oral testimony and eyewitness accounts of Jesus.

CHAPTER 6

Are the Bible Records Reliable?

THE NEW TESTAMENT PROVIDES THE PRIMARY HISTORICAL source for information about Jesus. Because of this, in the past two centuries many critics have attacked the reliability of the biblical documents. There seems to be a constant barrage of charges that have no historical foundation or that have been proved invalid by archaeological discoveries and research.

While I (Josh) was lecturing at Arizona State University, a professor who had brought his literature class approached me after an outdoor "free speech" lecture. He said, "Mr. McDowell, you are basing all your claims about Christ on a second-century document that is obsolete. I showed in class today that the New Testament was written so long after Christ lived that it could not be accurate in what it recorded."

I replied, "Sir, I understand your view, and I know the writings on which you base it. But the fact is, those writings have been proven wrong by more recently discovered documents that clearly show the New Testament to have been written within a generation of the time of Christ."

The source of that professor's opinions about the records concerning Jesus was the writings of the German critic Ferdinand Christian Baur. F. C. Baur assumed that most of the New Testament Scriptures were not written until late in the second century AD from myths and legends that had developed during the lengthy interval between the lifetime of Jesus and the time these accounts were set down in writing.

Twentieth-century archaeological discoveries confirmed the accuracy of the New Testament manuscripts.

By the twentieth century, however, archaeological discoveries had confirmed the accuracy of the New Testament manuscripts. Early papyri manuscripts (the John Rylands manuscript, AD 130; the Chester Beatty Papyri, AD 155; and the Bodmer Papyri II, AD 200) bridged the gap between the time of Christ and existing manuscripts from later dates.

Millar Burrows, for many years professor of biblical theology at Yale Divinity School, says:

> Another result of comparing New Testament Greek with the language of the papyri [discoveries] is an increase of confidence in the accurate transmission of the text of the New Testament itself.[1]

Such findings as these have increased scholarly confidence in the Bible.

William F. Albright, who was the world's foremost biblical archaeologist, writes,

> We can already say emphatically that there is no longer any solid basis for dating any book of the New Testament after about A.D. 80, two full generations before the date between 130 and 150 given by the more radical New Testament critics of today.[2]

He reiterates this view in an interview for *Christianity Today*.

> In my opinion, every book of the New Testament was written by a baptized Jew between the forties and the eighties of the first century A.D. (very probably sometime between about A.D. 50 and 75).[3]

Sir William Ramsay, one of the greatest archaeologists ever to have lived, was a student of the German historical school, which taught that the book of Acts was a product of the mid-second century AD and not of the first century as it purports to be. After reading modern criticism about the book of Acts, Ramsay became convinced that it was not a trustworthy account of the facts of its time (AD 50) and therefore was unworthy of consideration by a historian. So in his research on the history of Asia Minor, Ramsay paid little attention to the New Testament. His investigation, however, eventually compelled him to consider the writings of Luke, the author of the book of Acts. The archaeologist observed the meticulous accuracy of the historical details, and gradually his attitude toward the book of Acts began to change. He was forced to conclude that

> Luke is a historian of the first rank. . . . This author should be placed along with the very greatest of historians.[4]

Because of the book's accuracy even on the minutest details, Ramsay finally conceded that Acts could not be a second-century document but belonged rather to the mid-first century.

Many liberal scholars are being forced to consider earlier dates for the New Testament. The late Anglican bishop John A. T. Robinson's conclusions in his book *Redating the New Testament* are startlingly radical. His research led to his conviction that the whole of the New Testament was written before the fall of Jerusalem in AD 70.[5]

> **What Do You Think?**
> *Have there been any biblical archaeological discoveries in recent years that grabbed your attention? Why do these discoveries always get worldwide headlines?*

Today the form critics, scholars who analyze the ancient literary forms and oral traditions behind the biblical writings, say that the material was passed by word of mouth until it was written down in the form of the Gospels. Even though they now admit the period of transmission to be much shorter than previously believed, they still conclude that the Gospel accounts took on the forms of folk literature (legends, tales, myths, and parables).

One of the major charges against the form critics' concept of oral tradition development is that the period between the New Testament events and the recording of them is not long enough to have allowed the alterations from fact to legend that these critics allege. Speaking of the brevity of this interval, Simon Kistemaker, professor of New Testament emeritus at Reformed Theological Seminary, writes:

> Normally, the accumulation of folklore among people of primitive culture takes many generations; it is a gradual process spread over centuries of time. But in conformity with the thinking of the form critic, we must conclude that the Gospel stories were produced and collected within little more than one generation. In terms of the form-critical approach, the formation of the individual Gospel units must be understood as a telescoped project with accelerated course of action.[6]

A. H. McNeile, former Regius Professor of Divinity at the University of Dublin, challenges form criticism's concept of oral tradition. He points out that form critics do not deal with the tradition of Jesus' words as closely as they should. In the Jewish culture it was important that a teacher's actual words were carefully preserved and passed down. For example, 1 Corinthians 7:10, 12, and 25 show the existence of a genuine tradition and the careful preservation of it. It was customary for a Jewish student to memorize a rabbi's teaching. A good pupil was like "a plastered cistern that loses not a drop" (Mishna, Aboth, ii, 8). If we rely on Anglican Bible scholar C. F. Burney's theory in *The Poetry of Our Lord*, we can assume that much of the Lord's teaching is in Aramaic poetical form, making it easy to memorize.[7] It is impossible that in such a culture a tradition of legends that did not conform to actual facts could have developed in such a short time.

Other scholars concur. Paul L. Maier, professor of ancient history at Western Michigan University, writes: "Arguments that Christianity hatched its Easter myth over a lengthy period of time or that the sources were written many years after the event are simply not factual."[8] Analyzing form criticism, Albright writes: "Only modern scholars who lack both historical method and perspective can spin such a web of speculation as that with which form critics have surrounded the Gospel tradition." Albright's own conclusion was that "a period of twenty to fifty years is too slight to permit any appreciable corruption of the essential content and even of the specific wording of the sayings of Jesus."[9] Jeffery L. Sheler, religion writer for *US News & World Report*, writes, "The Bible and its sources remain firmly grounded in history."[10]

> **In the Jewish culture it was important that a teacher's actual words were carefully preserved and passed down.**

Four Gospels or Twenty Gospels?

In his wildly successful thriller *The Da Vinci Code*, author Dan Brown makes the audacious claim that "More than eighty gospels were considered for the New Testament, and yet only a relative few were chosen for inclusion—Matthew, Mark, Luke, and John among them."[11] In the 1990s, the Jesus Seminar published a book entitled *The Complete Gospels* that claims to be the first release of twenty known gospels from the early Christian era. The most notable of these are the gospels of Thomas, Judas, Philip, Peter, and Mary. The implication is clear: these ancient texts reveal a different view of Jesus just as valid as the time-honored tradition of the church. Is there any truth to these claims? Have the four Gospels lost their privileged status as unique purveyors of the life and ministry of Jesus? Are these recently uncovered gospels transforming our understanding of Christianity?

As extraordinary and dramatic as such claims may seem, they simply fall apart under the weight of historical analysis. In *Hidden Gospels*, historian Philip Jenkins concludes that the "idea that the various noncanonical gospels are equally valid witnesses to Christian antiquity is deeply flawed."[12] The most serious challenge to the status of these other gospels is their late dating. While the four Gospels were all written within the first century, all evidence points to these other gospels being composed between AD 120 and 250, at least three generations removed from the life of Christ.

Because these texts are written so much later than the four traditional Gospels, it is unlikely that they reveal any novel information about the historical Jesus. Thus, New Testament professor Craig A. Evans concludes, "The scholarly track record with respect to the use of these extracanonical Gospels is, frankly, embarrassing. . . . We have found that these extracanonical

> **What Do You Think?**
> *Do you give any credence to books, articles, or TV documentaries with extrabiblical information about the credibility and historicity of Jesus? How would you compare the historical evidence for Jesus with that for other well-known persons?*

Gospels do not offer early, reliable tradition, independent of what we possess in the New Testament Gospels."[13]

Often non-Christians tell me that we can't trust what the Bible says. "Why, it was written more than two thousand years ago. It's full of errors and discrepancies," they say. I reply that I believe I can trust the Scriptures. Then I describe an incident that took place during a lecture in a history class. I stated that I believed there was more evidence for the reliability of the New Testament than for almost any other ten pieces of classical literature put together.

The professor sat over in the corner snickering, as if to say, "Oh, come on now, you can't believe that." I asked him what he was snickering about. He replied, "I can't believe you have the audacity to claim in a history class that the New Testament is reliable. That's ridiculous!"

Wanting to find common ground for a gentlemanly discussion, I asked him this question: "Tell me, sir, as a historian, what are the tests that you apply to any piece of historical writing to determine its accuracy and reliability?" I was amazed that he did not have any such tests. In fact, I have yet to get a positive answer to this question. "I have some tests," I answered. I told him that I strongly believe we should test the historical reliability of the Scripture by the same rigorous criteria that we apply to all historical documents. Military historian Chauncey Sanders lists and explains the three basic principles of historiography: the *bibliographical* test, the *internal evidence* test, and the *external evidence* test.[14] Let's examine each one.

Bibliographical Test

The bibliographical test is an examination of the textual transmission by which ancient documents reach us from the past. In other words, since we don't have the original manuscripts, we have to ask the questions: How reliable are the copies we have? How many manuscripts have survived? How consistent are they? What is the time interval between the original and the extant copies?

We can appreciate the tremendous wealth of manuscript authority for the New Testament by comparing it to textual material available to support other notable ancient writings.

The history of Thucydides (460–400 BC) is available to us from only eight manuscripts dated about AD 900, almost thirteen hundred years after he wrote. The manuscripts of the history of Herodotus are likewise late and scarce. And yet, as F. F. Bruce, Rylands Professor of Biblical Criticism and Exegesis at the University of Manchester, concludes,

> "No classical scholar would listen to an argument that the authenticity of Herodotus or Thucydides is in doubt because the earliest manuscripts of their works which are of use to us are over 1,300 years later than the originals."
> —*F. F. Bruce*

> No classical scholar would listen to an argument that the authenticity of Herodotus or Thucydides is in doubt because the earliest manuscripts of their works which are of use to us are over 1,300 years later than the originals.[15]

Aristotle wrote his poetics around 343 BC, and yet the earliest copy we have is dated AD 1100 (a gap of almost fourteen hundred years), and only forty-nine manuscripts exist.

Caesar composed his history of the Gallic Wars between 58 and 50 BC, and its manuscript authority rests on nine or ten copies dating one thousand years after his death.

Bruce Metzger, author or editor of fifty books on the manuscript authority of the New Testament looks at other first-century notables:

> Consider Tacitus, the Roman historian who wrote his *Annals of Imperial Rome* in about A.D. 116. His first six books exist today in only one manuscript, and it was copied about A.D. 850. Books eleven through sixteen are in another manuscript dating from the eleventh century. Books seven through ten are lost. So there is a long gap between the time that Tacitus sought his information and wrote it down and the only existing copies.
>
> With regard to the first-century historian Josephus, we have nine Greek manuscripts of his work *The Jewish War*, and these copies were written in the tenth, eleventh, and twelfth centuries. There is a Latin translation from the fourth century and medieval Russian materials from the eleventh or twelfth century.

"The quantity of New Testament material," confesses Metzger, 'is almost embarrassing in comparison with other works of antiquity."[16]

When I first wrote this book in 1977, I was able to document forty-six hundred Greek manuscripts of the

Bible, abundantly more source material than exists for any other book written in antiquity. As of this writing, even more Greek manuscripts have been found, and I can now document more than fifty-six hundred of them.

Daniel Wallace, professor of New Testament studies at Dallas Theological Seminary and one of the world's leading authorities on the Greek text and New Testament manuscripts, states,

> Well over 200 biblical manuscripts (90 of which are New Testament) were discovered in the Sinai in 1975 when a hidden compartment of St. George's Tower was uncovered. Some of these manuscripts are quite ancient. They [the recent manuscript discoveries] all confirm that the transmission of the New Testament has been accomplished in relative purity and that God knows how to preserve the text from destruction. In addition to the manuscripts, there are 50,000 fragments sealed in boxes. About 30 separate New Testament manuscripts have been identified in the fragments, and scholars believe there may be many more.[17]

What Do You Think?

Do you—or someone you know—believe that because the Bible text is ancient it can't be trusted? Are there other nonbiblical ancient texts that you have no problem trusting?

When it comes to the manuscript authority of the New Testament, the abundance of material is truly remarkable

Josh McDowell & Sean McDowell

in contrast to the manuscript availability of other classic texts. After the early papyri manuscript discoveries that bridged the gap between the times of Christ and the second century, a profusion of other manuscripts came to light. More than twenty thousand copies of New Testament manuscripts are in existence as of 2009. The *Iliad*, which is second to the New Testament in manuscript authority, has only 643 manuscripts in existence.

More than twenty thousand copies of New Testament manuscripts are in existence as of 2009. The *Iliad*, second to the New Testament in manuscript authority, has only 643 manuscripts in existence.

Jewish scholar Jacob Klausner says, "If we had ancient sources like those in the Gospels for the history of Alexander or Caesar, we should not cast any doubt upon them whatsoever."[18]

Sir Frederic Kenyon, former director and principal librarian at the British Museum and whose authority on ancient manuscripts is second to none, concludes:

> The interval then between the dates of original composition and the earliest extant evidence becomes so small as to be in fact negligible, and the last foundation for any doubt that the Scriptures have come down to us substantially as they were written has now been removed. Both the authenticity and the general integrity of the books of the New Testament may be regarded as finally established.[19]

Others agree. Anglican bishop and New Testament historian Stephen Neill argues that "we have a far better and more reliable text of the New Testament than of any other ancient work whatever."[20]

Craig Blomberg, former senior research fellow at Cambridge University in England and now professor of New Testament at Denver Seminary, explains that the texts of the New Testament "have been preserved in far greater number and with much more care than have any other ancient documents." Blomberg concludes that "97–99% of the New Testament can be reconstructed beyond any reasonable doubt."[21]

New Testament Greek scholar J. Harold Greenlee adds:

> Since scholars accept as generally trustworthy the writings of the ancient classics even though the earliest manuscripts were written so long after the original writings and the number of extant manuscripts is in many instances so small, it is clear that the reliability of the text of the New Testament is likewise assured.[22]

The application of the bibliographical test to the New Testament assures us that it has more manuscript authority than any other piece of literature from antiquity. If we add to that authority the more than 130 years of intensive New Testament textual criticism, we can conclude that an authentic New Testament text has been established.

What about Biblical Variants?

In 2005, textual critic Bart Ehrman created a firestorm of controversy with the release of his best-selling book,

Misquoting Jesus. His claim was simple: the biblical manuscripts have so many errors that we cannot recover the original text. Some of these mistakes were accidental, claims Ehrman, while others were intentional. Either way, the New Testament as we know it today cannot be trusted.

A key point Ehrman raises is the 300,000 to 400,000 variants among New Testament manuscripts. A textual variant is any time the New Testament manuscripts have alternative wordings. Given that the Greek New Testament of today has roughly 138,000 words, the idea that there are two to three times as many variants as words is quite disturbing. Yet one needs to realize that the large number of variants is a direct result of the extremely large number of New Testament manuscripts that we have. There are no other works of antiquity that come close to the wealth of New Testament manuscripts available. The more manuscripts you possess, the more variants; the fewer the manuscripts, the fewer variants. But this is not the whole picture. When the variants are looked at more closely, a very different story emerges.

By far the most significant category of variants is spelling differences. The name John, for example, may be spelled with one n or with two. Clearly, a variation of this sort in no way jeopardizes the meaning of the text. Spelling differences account for roughly 75 percent of all variants.[23] That's between 225,000 and 300,000 of all the variants! Another large category of variants consists of the synonyms used across manuscripts. For instance, some manuscripts may refer to Jesus by his proper name, while others may say "Lord" or "he." Such differences hardly call the meaning of the text into question.

When all variations are considered, roughly one percent involve the meaning of the text. But even this fact can be overstated. For instance, there is disagreement about whether 1 John 1:4 should be translated, "Thus we are writing these things so that *our* joy may be complete" or "Thus we are writing these things so that *your* joy may be complete." While this disagreement does involve the meaning of the passage, it in no way jeopardizes a central doctrine of the Christian faith. This is why the authors of *Reinventing Jesus* conclude, "The short answer to the question of what theological truths are at stake in these variants is—none."[24] As we've seen in this chapter, we can have a high degree of confidence in the New Testament writings.

Internal Evidence Test

The bibliographical test determines only that the text we have now is what was originally recorded. One has still to determine not only whether that original written record is credible but also to what extent it is credible. That is the task of internal criticism, which is the second test of historicity cited by Chauncey Sanders.

Apologist John W. Montgomery reminds us that

> historical and literary scholarship continues to follow Aristotle's eminently just dictum that the benefit of doubt is to be given to the document itself, not arrogated by the critic to himself.

Montgomery continues:

> This means that one must listen to the claims of the document under analysis, and not assume

fraud or error unless the author disqualifies himself by contradictions or known factual inaccuracies.[25]

Louis Gottschalk, former professor of history at the University of Chicago, outlines his historical method in a guide used by many for historical investigation. Gottschalk points out that the ability of the writer or the witness to tell the truth is helpful to historians in their effort to determine credibility, "even if it is contained in a document obtained by force or fraud, or is otherwise impeachable, or is based on hearsay evidence, or is from an interested witness."[26]

This ability to tell the truth is closely related to the witness's nearness both geographically and chronologically to the events recorded. The New Testament accounts of the life and teaching of Jesus were recorded by men who had either been eyewitnesses themselves or who related the accounts of eyewitnesses of the actual events or teachings of Christ. Consider these statements from the New Testament:

> Many people have set out to write accounts about the events that have been fulfilled among us. They used the eyewitness reports circulating among us from the early disciples. Having carefully investigated everything from the beginning, I also have decided to write a careful account for you, most honorable Theophilus, so you can be certain of the truth of everything you were taught.
>
> LUKE 1:1-4

Scholars acknowledge Luke's historical accuracy. "The general consensus of both liberal and conservative scholars is that Luke is very accurate as a historian," explains John

McRay, professor of New Testament and archaeology at Wheaton College.

> He's erudite, he's eloquent, his Greek approaches classical quality, he writes as an educated man, and archaeological discoveries are showing over and over again that Luke is accurate in what he has to say.[27]

Luke is not the only biblical writer concerned with accurate reporting. Consider some other accounts:

> We were not making up clever stories when we told you about the powerful coming of our Lord Jesus Christ. We saw his majestic splendor with our own eyes.   2 PETER 1:16

> We proclaim to you what we ourselves have actually seen and heard so that you may have fellowship with us. And our fellowship is with the Father and with his Son, Jesus Christ.   1 JOHN 1:3

> This report is from an eyewitness giving an accurate account. He speaks the truth so that you also can believe.   JOHN 19:35

> During the forty days after his crucifixion, he appeared to the apostles from time to time, and he proved to them in many ways that he was actually alive. And he talked to them about the Kingdom of God.   ACTS 1:3

> We cannot stop telling about everything we have seen and heard.   ACTS 4:20

After examining just six eyewitness testimonies (Matthew, John, Paul, Peter, James, and Jude), apologetics professor Lynn Gardner concludes that in comparison to the evidence of other literature of antiquity, "we have far better sources for our knowledge of Jesus of Nazareth."[28]

> **What Do You Think?**
> *After reading the six biblical eyewitness accounts above, what words or phrases do they use that make you carefully consider their claims? What emotion seems to reverberate in these accounts?*

This close proximity of the writers to the events they recorded gives extremely effective certification to the accuracy of eyewitnesses. Their memories are still vivid. However, the historian must deal with eyewitnesses who, though competent to tell the truth, deliberately or unwittingly give false accounts.

Dr. Norman Geisler, founder of Southern Evangelical Seminary, summarizes the eyewitness testimony:

> Both the vast number of the independent eyewitnesses accounts of Jesus . . . as well as the nature and integrity of the witnesses themselves leave beyond reasonable doubt the reliability of the apostolic testimony about Christ.[29]

The New Testament accounts of Christ were being circulated within the lifetimes of his contemporaries. These people whose lives overlapped his could certainly confirm or deny the accuracy of the accounts. In advocating their case for the gospel, the apostles had appealed (even when confronting their most severe opponents) to common knowledge concerning Jesus. They not only said, "Look, we saw this" or "We heard that," but they turned the tables and said right in the face of adverse critics, "You also know about these things. You saw them. You yourselves know about it." But listen to the challenge in the following passages:

> Men of Israel, listen to these words: Jesus the Nazarene, a man attested to you by God with miracles and wonders and signs which God performed through Him in your midst, just as you yourselves know.   ACTS 2:22 (NASB)

> Suddenly, Festus shouted, "Paul, you are insane. Too much study has made you crazy!" But Paul replied, "I am not insane, Most Excellent Festus. What I am saying is the sober truth. And King Agrippa knows about these things. I speak boldy, for I am sure these events are all familiar to him, for they were not done in a corner!"   ACTS 26:24-26

One had better be careful when he says to his opposition, "You know this also," because if there isn't common knowledge and agreement of the details, the challenge will be shoved right back down his throat.

Concerning this primary-source value of the New Testament records, F. F. Bruce says:

> It was not only friendly eyewitnesses that the early preachers had to reckon with; there were others

less well disposed who were also conversant with the main facts of the ministry and death of Jesus. The disciples could not afford to risk inaccuracies (not to speak of willful manipulation of the facts), which would at once be exposed by those who would be only too glad to do so. On the contrary, one of the strong points in the original apostolic preaching is the confident appeal to the knowledge of the hearers; they not only said, "We are witnesses of these things," but also, "As you yourselves also know" (Acts 2:22). Had there been any tendency to depart from the facts in any material respect, the possible presence of hostile witnesses in the audience would have served as a further corrective.[30]

> **The New Testament accounts of Christ were being circulated within the lifetimes of his contemporaries. These people whose lives overlapped his could certainly confirm or deny the accuracy of the accounts.**

Lawrence J. McGinley of Saint Peter's College comments on the value of hostile witnesses in relationship to recorded events:

First of all, eyewitnesses of the events in question were still alive when the tradition had been completely formed; and among those eyewitnesses were bitter enemies of the new religious movement. Yet the tradition claimed to narrate a series of well-known deeds and publicly taught doctrines at a time when false statements could, and would, be challenged.[31]

This is why renowned historian David Hackett Fischer, professor of history at Brandeis University, explains that the eyewitness testimony of the apostles is "the best relevant evidence."[32]

New Testament scholar Robert Grant of the University of Chicago concludes:

> At the time they [the synoptic gospels] were written or may be supposed to have been written, there were eyewitnesses and their testimony was not completely disregarded. . . . This means that the gospels must be regarded as largely reliable witnesses to the life, death, and the resurrection of Jesus.[33]

Historian Will Durant, who was trained in the discipline of historical investigation and spent his life analyzing records of antiquity, writes:

> Despite the prejudices and theological misconceptions of the evangelists, they record many incidents that mere inventors would have concealed—the competition of the apostles for high places in the Kingdom, their flight after Jesus' arrest, Peter's denial, the failure of Christ to work miracles in Galilee, the references of some auditors to his possible insanity, his early uncertainty as to his mission, his confessions of ignorance as to the

future, his moments of bitterness, his despairing cry on the cross; no one reading these scenes can doubt the reality of the figure behind them. That a few simple men should in one generation have invented so powerful and appealing a personality, so lofty an ethic, and so inspiring a vision of human brotherhood, would be a miracle far more incredible than any recorded in the Gospels. After two centuries of Higher Criticism the outlines of the life, character, and teaching of Christ remain reasonably clear, and constitute the most fascinating feature in the history of Western man.[34]

External Evidence Test

The third test of historicity is that of external evidence. The issue here is whether other historical material confirms or denies the internal testimony of the documents themselves. In other words, what sources, apart from the literature under analysis, substantiate the document's accuracy, reliability, and authenticity?

Louis Gottschalk argues that "conformity or agreement with other known historical or scientific facts is often the decisive test of evidence, whether of one or more witnesses."[35]

Two friends and disciples of the apostle John confirm the internal evidence that appears in John's accounts. The first was Papias, bishop of Hierapolos (AD 130). The historian Eusebius preserves the writings of Papias as follows:

The Elder [apostle John] used to say this also: "Mark, having been the interpreter of Peter, wrote down accurately all that he [Peter] mentioned, whether sayings or doings of Christ, not, however, in order. For he was neither a hearer nor a companion of the Lord; but afterwards, as I said, he accompanied Peter, who adapted his teachings as necessity required, not as though he were making a compilation of the sayings of the Lord. So then Mark made no mistake, writing down in this way some things

The third test of historicity is that of external evidence—whether other historical material confirms or denies the internal testimony of the documents themselves.

as he mentioned them; for he paid attention to this one thing, not to omit anything that he had heard, not to include any false statement among them."[36]

The second friend of John was one of his disciples, Polycarp, who became bishop of Smyrna and had been a Christian for eighty-six years. Polycarp's student Irenaeus, later bishop of Lyons (AD 180) wrote of what he learned from Polycarp (John's disciple):

Matthew published his gospel among the Hebrews [i.e., Jews] in their own tongue, when Peter and Paul were preaching the gospel in Rome and founding the church there. After their departure [i.e., death, which strong tradition places at the time of the Neronian persecution in AD 64], Mark, the disciple and interpreter of Peter, himself handed down to us in writing the substance of

Peter's preaching. Luke, the follower of Paul, set down in a book the gospel preached by his teacher. Then John, the disciple of the Lord, who also leaned on his breast [this is a reference to John 13:25 and 21:20] himself produced his Gospel, while he was living at Ephesus in Asia.[37]

In *The Historical Jesus: Ancient Evidence for the Life of Christ*, Gary Habermas meticulously documents the extrabiblical evidence for the historical Jesus. Greek, Roman, and Jewish documents offer support for key elements of the life, ministry, and death of Jesus. This evidence includes notable examples such as (1) the crucifixion of Jesus by the Romans; (2) worship of Jesus as deity; (3) belief in the resurrection of Jesus; (4) Jesus being the brother of James; and (5) the empty tomb. Habermas concludes that "ancient extrabiblical sources do present a surprisingly large amount of detail concerning both the life of Jesus and the nature of early Christianity."[38]

> **What Do You Think?**
> Even with archaeological evidence, critics often state that the Scriptures are not historically accurate. Why do you think that's the case? Is there any evidence that would be irrefutable for you?

Archaeology also provides powerful external evidence. It contributes to biblical criticism, not in the area of inspiration and revelation, but by providing evidence of accuracy concerning the events recorded. Archaeologist Joseph Free writes: "Archaeology has confirmed countless passages which have been rejected by critics as unhistorical or contradictory to known facts."[39]

We have already seen how archaeology caused Sir William Ramsay to change his initial negative convictions about the historicity of Luke and conclude that the book of Acts was accurate in its description of the geography, antiquities, and society of Asia Minor.

F. F. Bruce notes that "where Luke has been suspected of inaccuracy, and accuracy has been vindicated by some inscriptional [external] evidence, it may be legitimate to say that archaeology has confirmed the New Testament record."[40]

A. N. Sherwin-White, a classical historian, writes that "for Acts the confirmation of historicity is overwhelming." He continues by saying that "any attempt to reject its basic historicity even in matters of detail must now appear absurd. Roman historians have long taken it for granted."[41]

After personally trying to shatter the historicity and validity of the Scriptures, I have been forced to conclude that they are historically trustworthy. If one discards the Bible as unreliable historically, then he or she must discard all the literature of antiquity. No other document has as much evidence to confirm its reliability. One problem I face constantly is the desire on the part of many to apply one standard to test secular literature and another to the Bible. We must apply the same standard, whether the literature under investigation is secular or religious. Having done this myself, I am convinced that the Bible is trustworthy and historically reliable in its witness about Jesus.

If one discards the Bible as unreliable historically, then he or she must discard all the literature of antiquity.

Clark H. Pinnock, professor emeritus of systematic theology at McMaster Divinity College, states:

> There exists no document from the ancient world witnessed by so excellent a set of textual and historical testimonies, and offering so superb an array of historical data on which an intelligent decision may be made. An honest [person] cannot dismiss a source of this kind. Skepticism regarding the historical credentials of Christianity is based on an irrational [i.e., antisupernatural] bias.[42]

Douglas Groothuis, associate professor of philosophy and head of the philosophy of religion department at Denver Seminary, points out that "the New Testament is better attested by ancient manuscripts than any other piece of ancient literature."[43]

CHAPTER 7

Who Would Die for a Lie?

THOSE WHO CHALLENGE CHRISTIANITY OFTEN OVERLOOK one area of evidence: the transformation of Jesus' apostles. The radically changed lives of these men give us solid testimony for the validity of Christ's claims.

Since the Christian faith is historical, our knowledge of it must rely heavily on testimony, both written and oral. Without such testimony, we have no window to any historical event, Christian or otherwise. In fact, all history is essentially a knowledge of the past based on testimony. If reliance on such testimony seems to give history too shaky a foundation, we must ask, How else can we learn of the past? How can we know that Napoleon lived? None of us was alive in his time period. We didn't see him or meet him. We must rely on testimony.

Our knowledge of history has one inherent problem: Can we trust that the testimony is reliable? Since our knowledge of Christianity is based on testimony given in the distant past, we must ask whether we can depend on its accuracy. Were the original oral testimonies about Jesus trustworthy? Can we trust them to have conveyed correctly what Jesus said and did? I believe we can.

I can trust the apostles' testimonies because eleven of those men died martyrs' deaths because they stood solid for two truths: Christ's deity and his resurrection. These men were tortured and flogged, and most finally suffered death by some of the cruelest methods then known:[1]

1. Peter, originally called Simon, was crucified.
2. Andrew was crucified.
3. James, son of Zebedee, was killed by the sword.
4. John, son of Zebedee, died a natural death.
5. Philip was crucified.
6. Bartholomew was crucified.
7. Thomas was killed by a spear.
8. Matthew was killed by the sword.
9. James, son of Alphaeus, was crucified.
10. Thaddaeus was killed by arrows.
11. Simon, the zealot, was crucified.

The perspective I often hear is, "Well, these men died for a lie. Many people have done that. So what does it prove?"

Yes, many people have died for a lie, but they did so believing it was the truth. What was the case with the disciples? If the Resurrection had not happened, obviously the disciples would have known it. I can find no way that these particular men could have been deceived. Therefore they not only would have died for a lie—here's the catch—but they would have known it was a lie. It would be hard to find a group of men anywhere in history who would die for a lie if they knew it was a lie.

Let's look at several factors that will help us understand the factual truth of what they believed.

1. They Were Eyewitnesses

In his 2006 scholarly book *Jesus and the Eyewitnesses*, New Testament professor Richard Bauckham demonstrates that the four Gospels provide reliable testimony that can be traced back to the eyewitnesses themselves.[2]

The apostles wrote and other disciples spoke as actual eyewitnesses to the events they described. Peter said: "We were not making up clever stories when we told you about the powerful coming of our Lord Jesus Christ. We saw his majestic splendor with our own eyes" (2 Peter 1:16). The apostles certainly knew the difference between myth or legend and reality.

In his first letter, John emphasized the eyewitness aspect of their knowledge, explaining how he and the other apostles got their information about what Jesus "did" and "said": "We proclaim to you the one who existed from the beginning, whom we have heard and seen. We saw him with our own eyes and touched him with our own hands. He is the Word of life. This one who is life itself was revealed to us, and we have seen him. And now we testify and proclaim to you that he is the one who is eternal life. He was with the Father, and then he was

Throughout history, many people have died for what they thought was the truth. However, for Jesus' disciples—most of whom were martyrs for Christ—if the Resurrection had not happened, they would have known it.

revealed to us. We proclaim to you what we ourselves have actually seen and heard so that you may have fellowship with us. And our fellowship is with the Father and with his Son, Jesus Christ" (1 John 1:1-3). John began the last portion of his Gospel by saying that "The disciples saw Jesus do many other miraculous signs in addition to the ones recorded in this book" (John 20:30).

What Do You Think?

Is there anything or anyone that you would die for? Why do you feel that way?

Luke said, "Many people have set out to write accounts about the events that have been fulfilled among us. They used the eyewitness reports circulating among us from the early disciples. Having carefully investigated everything from the beginning, I also have decided to write a careful account for you" (Luke 1:1-3).

What Do You Think?

Have you ever been an eyewitness to something and later were asked to tell what you saw? Did people believe you? What makes someone a credible eyewitness?

Then in the book of Acts, Luke described the forty-day period after the Resurrection, when the followers of Jesus closely observed him: "In my first book I told you, Theophilus, about everything Jesus began to do and teach until the day he was taken up to heaven after giving his chosen apostles further instructions through the Holy Spirit. During the forty days after his crucifixion, he appeared to the apostles from time to time, and he proved to them in many ways that he was actually alive. And he talked to them about the Kingdom of God" (Acts 1:1-3).

The central theme of the following eyewitness testimonies is the resurrection of Jesus. The apostles were witnesses to his resurrected life.

2. They Had to Be Convinced

The apostles thought that when Jesus died, it was all over. When he was arrested, they went and hid (see Mark 14:50). When they were told the tomb was empty, they did not at first believe it (see Luke 24:11). Only after ample and convincing evidence did they believe. Then we have Thomas, who said he wouldn't believe that Christ was raised from the dead until he had put his finger into Christ's wounds. Thomas later died a martyr's death for Christ. Was he deceived? He bet his life that he was not.

Then there was Peter. He denied his Lord several times during Christ's trial and finally deserted him. But something turned this coward around. A short time after Christ's crucifixion and burial, Peter showed up in Jerusalem preaching boldly, under the threat of death, that Jesus was the Christ and had been resurrected. Finally, Peter was crucified (upside down, according to tradition). What could have turned this terrified deserter into such a bold lion for Jesus? Why was Peter suddenly willing to die for him? Was the apostle deceived? Hardly. The only explanation that satisfies me is what we read in 1 Corinthians 15:5, that after Christ's resurrection, "he was seen by Peter." Peter witnessed his Lord's resurrection, and he believed—to the extent that he was willing to die for his belief.

The classic example of a man convinced against his will was James, the brother of Jesus. (Although James wasn't one of the original Twelve [see Matthew 10:2-4], he was later recognized as an apostle [see Galatians 1:19], as were Paul and Barnabas [see Acts 14:14]). While Jesus was growing up and engaged in his ministry, James didn't believe that his brother was the Son of God (see John 7:5). No doubt James participated with his brothers in mocking Jesus, possibly saying things such as: "You want people to believe in you? Why don't you go up to Jerusalem and put on a big show with all your miracles and healings?" James must have felt humiliated that his brother was going around bringing shame and ridicule on the family name with all his wild claims: "I am the way, the truth, and the life. No one can come to the Father except through me" (John 14:6); "I am the vine; you are the branches" (John 15:5); "I am the good shepherd; I know my own sheep, and they know me" (John 10:14). What would you think if your brother went around the town saying such things?

What Do You Think?

For the most part, Jesus' siblings were resistant to what he was doing and saying. Traditionally, family members are often the most resistant to a change in a family member. Why do you think that is?

But something happened to James. After Jesus was crucified and buried, James was preaching in Jerusalem. His message was that Jesus died for our sins and was resurrected and is alive. Eventually James became a leading figure in the Jerusalem church and wrote a book, the Epistle of James. He began it by writing, "James, a slave [servant] of God and of the Lord Jesus Christ" (James 1:1). Eventually James was stoned to death on orders from Ananias, the high priest.[3] What could have changed James from an embarrassed scoffer to a man willing to die for his brother's deity? Was James deceived? No. The only plausible explanation is what we read in 1 Corinthians 15:7: "Then [after Christ's resurrection] he was seen by James." James saw the resurrected Christ and believed.

J. P. Moreland, professor of philosophy at the Talbot School of Theology, explains the significance of the fact that James, the brother of Jesus, eventually came to believe in Jesus as the Messiah:

> **What could have changed James from an embarrassed scoffer to a man willing to die for his brother's deity? He saw the resurrected Christ and believed.**

> The gospels tell us Jesus' family, including James, were embarrassed by what he was claiming to be. They didn't believe in him; they confronted him. In ancient Judaism it was highly embarrassing for a rabbi's family not to accept him. Therefore, the gospel writers would have no motive for fabricating this skepticism if it weren't true. Later the historian Josephus tells us that James, the brother of Jesus, who was the leader of the Jerusalem church, was stoned to death because of his belief in his brother. Why did James's life change? Paul tells us: the resurrected Jesus appeared to him. There's no other explanation.[4]

If the Resurrection were a lie, the apostles would have known it. Were they perpetuating a colossal hoax? Such a possibility is inconsistent with what we know about the moral quality of their lives. They personally condemned lying and stressed honesty. They encouraged people to know the truth. Historian Edward Gibbon in his famous work *The History of the Decline and Fall of the Roman Empire* gives the "purer but austere morality of the first Christians" as one of the five reasons for the rapid success of Christianity.[5] Michael Green, a senior research fellow at Wycliffe Hall, Oxford University, observes that the Resurrection

> was the belief that turned heartbroken followers of a crucified rabbi into the courageous witnesses and martyrs of the early church. This was the one belief that separated the followers of Jesus from the Jews and turned them into the community of the resurrection. You could imprison them, flog them, kill them, but you could not make them deny their conviction that "on the third day he rose again."[6]

3. They Became Courageous

The bold conduct of the apostles immediately after they were convinced of the Resurrection makes it highly unlikely that it was all a fraud. They became courageous almost overnight. After the Resurrection, Peter, who had denied Christ, stood up even at the threat of death and proclaimed that Jesus was alive. The authorities arrested the followers of Christ and beat them, yet they were soon back on the street speaking out about Jesus (see Acts 5:40-42). Their friends noticed their buoyancy, and their enemies noticed their courage. Remember that the apostles did not confine their boldness to obscure towns. They preached in Jerusalem.

Jesus' followers could not have faced torture and death

unless they were convinced of his resurrection. The unanimity of their message and their conduct was amazing. The odds against such a large group of people agreeing on such a controversial subject are enormous, yet all these men agreed on the truth of the Resurrection. If they were deceivers, it's hard to explain why at least one of them didn't break down under the pressure they endured.

> **Jesus' followers could not have faced torture and death unless they were convinced of his resurrection. The unanimity of their message and their conduct was amazing.**

Blaise Pascal, the French philosopher, writes:

> The allegation that the Apostles were imposters is quite absurd. Let us follow the charge to its logical conclusion. Let us picture those twelve men, meeting after the death of Christ, and entering into conspiracy to say that He has risen. That would have constituted an attack upon both the civil and the religious authorities. The heart of man is strangely given to fickleness and change; it is swayed by promises, tempted by material things. If any one of those men had yielded to temptations so alluring, or given way to the more compelling arguments of prison, torture, they would have all been lost.[7]

"When Jesus was crucified," explains J. P. Moreland,

> his followers were discouraged and depressed. They no longer had confidence that Jesus

had been sent by God, because they believed anyone crucified was accursed by God. They also had been taught that God would not let his Messiah suffer death. So they dispersed.

What Do You Think?

Do you admire people who are willing to die or have died for a cause? What attracts you to them? What scares you about them? Is there anything you can learn from them?

The Jesus movement was all but stopped in its tracks. Then, after a short period of time, we see them abandoning their occupations, regathering, and committing themselves to spreading a very specific message—that Jesus Christ was the Messiah of God who died on the cross, returned to life, and was seen alive by them. And they were willing to spend the rest of their lives proclaiming this, without any payoff from a human point of view. It's not as though there were a mansion awaiting them on the Mediterranean. They faced a life of hardship. They often went without food, slept exposed to the elements, were ridiculed, beaten, imprisoned. And finally, most of them were executed in torturous ways. For what? For good intentions? No, because they were convinced beyond a shadow of a doubt that they had seen Jesus Christ alive from the dead. What you can't explain is how this particular group of men came up with this particular belief without having had an experience of the resurrected Christ. There's no other adequate explanation.[8]

"How have they turned, almost overnight," asks Michael Green, "into the indomitable band of enthusiasts who braved opposition, cynicism, ridicule, hardship, prison, and death in three continents, as they preached everywhere Jesus and the resurrection?"[9]

One writer descriptively narrates the changes that occurred in the lives of the apostles:

> On the day of the crucifixion they were filled with sadness; on the first day of the week with gladness. At the crucifixion they were hopeless; on the first day of the week their hearts glowed with certainty and hope. When the message of the resurrection first came, they were incredulous and hard to be convinced, but once they became assured they never doubted again. What could account for the astonishing change in these men in so short a time? The mere removal of the body from the grave could never have transformed their spirits and characters. Three days are not enough for a legend to spring up which would so affect them. Time is needed for a process of legendary growth. It is a psychological fact that demands a full explanation. Think of the character of

Most of Jesus' followers were executed in torturous ways. For what? For good intentions? No, because they were convinced that they had seen Jesus Christ alive from the dead.

the witnesses, men and women who gave the world the highest ethical teaching it has ever known, and who even on the testimony of their enemies lived it out in their lives. Think of the psychological absurdity of picturing a little band of defeated cowards cowering in an upper room one day and a few days later transformed into a company that no persecution could silence—and then attempting to attribute this dramatic change to nothing more convincing than a miserable fabrication they were trying to foist upon the world. That simply wouldn't make sense.[10]

Church historian Kenneth Scott Latourette writes:

The effects of the resurrection and the coming of the Holy Spirit upon the disciples were . . . of major importance. From discouraged, disillusioned men and women who sadly looked back upon the days when they had hoped that Jesus "was he who should redeem Israel," they were made over into a company of enthusiastic witnesses.[11]

N. T. Wright, former professor of New Testament Studies at Oxford University in England, explains,

The historian has to say, "How do we explain the fact that this movement spread like wildfire with Jesus as the Messiah, even though Jesus had been crucified?" The answer has to be, it can only be, because He was raised from the dead.[12]

Paul Little, who was associate professor of evangelism at Trinity Evangelical Divinity School, asks:

> Are these men, who helped transform the moral structure of society, consummate liars or deluded madmen? These alternatives are harder to believe than the fact of the Resurrection, and there is no shred of evidence to support them.[13]

The steadfastness of the apostles even to death cannot be explained away. According to the *Encyclopaedia Britannica*, the philospher Origen records that Peter was crucified head downward. Church historian Herbert B. Workman describes the apostle's death:

> Thus Peter, as our Lord had prophesied, was "girt" by another, and "carried" out to die along the Aurelian Way, to a place hard by the gardens of Nero on the Vatican hill, where so many of his brethren had already suffered a cruel death. At his own request he was crucified head downwards, as unworthy to suffer like his Master.[14]

Harold Mattingly, who was an emeritus professor at the University of Leeds, writes in his history text: "The apostles, St. Peter and St. Paul, sealed their witnesses with their blood."[15] Tertullian writes that "no man would be willing to die unless he knew he had the truth."[16] Harvard law professor Simon Greenleaf, a man who lectured for years on how to break down a witness and determine whether or not he was lying, concludes:

The annals of military warfare afford scarcely an example of the like heroic constancy, patience, and unflinching courage. They had every possible motive to review carefully the grounds of their faith, and the evidence of the great facts and truths which they asserted.[17]

History professor Lynn Gardner rightly asks,

Why would they die for what they knew to be a lie? A person might be deceived and die for a falsehood. But the apostles were in a position to know the facts about Jesus' resurrection, and they still died for it.[18]

Tom Anderson, former president of the California Trial Lawyers Association, states,

Let's assume that the written accounts of His appearances to hundreds of people are false.

I want to pose a question. With an event so well publicized, don't you think that it's reasonable that one historian, one eyewitness, one antagonist would record for all time that he had seen Christ's body? . . . The silence of history is deafening when it comes to the testimony against the resurrection.[19]

The silence of history is deafening when it comes to the testimony against the resurrection.

J. P. Moreland points out, "No historian I know of doubts that Christianity started in Jerusalem just a few weeks after the death of Jesus in the presence of friendly and hostile eyewitnesses."[20] Furthermore, as William Lane Craig, research professor of philosophy at Talbot School of Theology, concludes,

> The site of Jesus' tomb was known to Christians and Jews alike. So if it weren't empty, it would be impossible for a movement founded on belief in the Resurrection to have come into existence in the same city where this man had been publicly executed and buried.[21]

The apostles went through the test of death to substantiate the veracity of what they were proclaiming. I believe I can trust their testimony more than that of most people I meet today. I grieve to find so many who lack enough conviction in their lives even to walk across the street for what they believe, much less to die for it.

What Do You Think?
How much credibility do the disciples deserve for offering their lives as confirmation of their beliefs? Could they have done anything more to show their sincerity?

CHAPTER 8

What Good Is a Dead Messiah?

MANY PEOPLE HAVE DIED FOR CAUSES THEY BELIEVE IN. In the 1960s many Buddhists burned themselves to death in order to bring world attention to injustices in Southeast Asia. In the early seventies a San Diego student burned himself to death protesting the Vietnam War. In September 2001 several Muslim extremists hijacked airliners and crashed them into the World Trade Center towers and the Pentagon to inflict damage on a nation they consider an enemy to their religion.

The apostles thought they had a good cause to die for, but they were stunned and disillusioned when that good cause died on the cross. They believed him to be the Messiah. They didn't think he could die. They were convinced that he was the one to set up the Kingdom of God and to rule over the people of Israel, and his death shattered their hopes.

In order to understand the apostles' relationship to Christ and why the Cross was so incomprehensible to them, you must grasp the national attitude about the Messiah at the time of Christ. His life and teachings were in tremendous conflict with the Jewish messianic understanding of that day. From childhood a Jew was taught that when the Messiah came, he would be a victorious, reigning political leader. He would free the Jews from bondage to the Romans and restore Israel to its rightful place as an independent nation that would shine like a beacon to all the world. A suffering Messiah was "completely foreign to the Jewish conception of messiahship."[1]

> **What Do You Think?**
>
> *Have you ever heard of someone having a messiah complex? Can you explain what that means? How does Jesus' behavior differ from what people expect from a messiah?*

Professor E. F. Scott of Union Theological Seminary gives his account of the expectant atmosphere at the time of Christ:

> The period was one of intense excitement. The religious leaders found it almost impossible to restrain the ardour of the people, who were waiting everywhere for the appearance of the promised Deliverer. This mood of expectancy had no doubt been heightened by the events of recent history.
>
> For more than a generation past, the Romans had been encroaching on Jewish freedom, and their measures of repression had stirred the spirit of patriotism to fiercer life. The dream of a

miraculous deliverance, and of a Messianic king who would effect it, assumed a new meaning in that critical time; but in itself it was nothing new. Behind the ferment of which we have evidence in the Gospels, we can discern a long period of growing anticipation.

To the people at large the Messiah remained what he had been to Isaiah and his contemporaries— the Son of David who would bring victory and prosperity to the Jewish nation. In the light of the Gospel references it can hardly be doubted that the popular conception of the Messiah was mainly national and political.[2]

Jewish scholar Joseph Klausner writes: "The Messiah became more and more not only a preeminent political ruler but also a man of preeminent moral qualities."[3]

Jacob Gartenhaus, founder of the International Board of Jewish Missions, reflects the prevailing Jewish beliefs in the time of Christ: "The Jews awaited the Messiah as the one who would deliver them from Roman oppression. . . . The messianic hope was basically for a national liberation."[4]

The *Jewish Encyclopedia* states that the Jews

yearned for the promised deliverer of the house of David, who would free them from the yoke of the hated foreign usurper, would put an end to the impious Roman rule, and would establish His own reign of peace and justice in its place.[5]

At that time the Jews were taking refuge in the promised Messiah. The apostles held the same beliefs as the people around them. As Millar Burrows of Yale University Divinity School states, "Jesus was so unlike what all Jews expected the son of David to be that His own disciples found it almost impossible to connect the idea of the Messiah with Him."[6] The disciples did not at all welcome Jesus' grave predictions about being crucified (see Luke 9:22). Scottish New Testament professor A. B. Bruce observes that there

> seems to have been the hope that He had taken too gloomy a view of the situation, and that His apprehensions would turn out groundless . . . a crucified Christ was a scandal and a contradiction to the apostles; quite as much as it continued to be to the majority of the Jewish people after the Lord had ascended to glory.[7]

Alfred Edersheim, once Grinfield Lecturer on the Septuagint at Oxford University, is right in concluding that "the most unlike thing to Christ were his times."[8] The reality of the person was utterly at odds with the heightened expectations of the day.

We can easily see in the New Testament the apostles' attitude toward Christ. Everything about him met their expectation of a reigning Messiah. After Jesus told them that he had to go to Jerusalem and suffer, James and John ignored the gloomy prediction and asked him to promise that in his Kingdom they could sit at his right and his left (see Mark 10:32-38). What type of Messiah were they thinking of—a suffering, crucified Messiah? No. They saw Jesus as a political ruler. He indicated that they had misunderstood what he had to do; they didn't know what they were asking. When he explicitly predicted his suffering and crucifixion, the idea was so foreign to the apostles' mind-set that they couldn't figure out what he meant (see Luke 18:31-34).

What Do You Think?

Have any of your ideas of who Jesus was been shattered? Been confirmed? Why do you think the disciples had so much difficulty knowing exactly who he was?

Because of their background and training in the general Jewish messianic expectation, they thought they were in on a good thing. Then came Calvary. All hopes that Jesus was their Messiah died on the cross. They returned to their homes, discouraged that all those years with Jesus had been wasted.

George Eldon Ladd, former professor of New Testament at Fuller Theological Seminary, writes:

> This is also why his disciples forsook him when he was taken captive. Their minds were so completely imbued with the idea of a conquering Messiah whose role it was to subdue his enemies that when they saw him broken and bleeding under the scourging, a helpless prisoner in the hands of

Pilate, and when they saw him led away, nailed to a cross to die as a common criminal, all their messianic hopes for Jesus were shattered. It is a sound psychological fact that we hear only what we are prepared to hear. Jesus' predictions of his suffering and death fell on deaf ears. The disciples, in spite of his warnings, were unprepared for it.[9]

But a few weeks after the Crucifixion, in spite of their former doubts, the disciples were in Jerusalem, proclaiming Jesus as Savior and Lord, the Messiah of the Jews. The only reasonable explanation I can see for this change is what I read in 1 Corinthians 15:5: "He was seen by Peter and then by the Twelve [apostles]." What else could have caused the despondent disciples to go out and suffer and die for a crucified Messiah? Jesus "appeared to the apostles from time to time, and he proved to them in many ways that he was actually alive. And he talked to them about the Kingdom of God" (Acts 1:3).

The Jews' national patriotism had led them to look for a Messiah to save their nation. What came instead was a Messiah who would save all of humanity from the eternal consequences of sin.

These men learned the truth about Jesus' identity as the Messiah. The Jews had misunderstood. Their national patriotism had led them to look for a Messiah to save their nation. What came instead was a Messiah to save the world. A Messiah who would save not merely one nation from political oppression but all of humanity from the eternal consequences of sin. The apostles' vision had been too small. Suddenly they saw the larger truth.

Yes, many people have died for a good cause, but the good cause of the apostles had died on the cross. At least, that is what they first thought. Only their contact with Christ after the Resurrection convinced these men that he was indeed the Messiah. To this they testified not only with their lips and lives but also with their deaths.

What Do You Think?

Have you ever had your expectations radically overturned? How do you think the disciples felt the very moment they realized Jesus was the risen Messiah?

CHAPTER 9

Did You Hear What Happened to Saul?

JACK, A CHRISTIAN FRIEND OF MINE WHO HAS SPOKEN AT many universities, arrived at a campus one morning to discover that the students had arranged for him to have a public discussion that night with the "university atheist." His opponent was an eloquent philosophy professor who was extremely antagonistic to Christianity. Jack was to speak first. He discussed various proofs for the resurrection of Jesus as well as the conversion of the apostle Paul, and then he gave his personal testimony about how Christ had changed his life when he was a university student.

When the philosophy professor got up to speak, he was quite nervous. He couldn't refute the evidence for the Resurrection or Jack's personal testimony, so he attacked the apostle Paul's radical conversion to Christianity. He used the argument that "people can often become so psychologically involved in what they're combating that they end up embracing it."

My friend smiled gently and responded, "You'd better be careful, sir, or you're liable to become a Christian."

The story of the apostle Paul is one of the most influential testimonies to Christianity. Saul of Tarsus, perhaps the most rabid antagonist of early Christianity, became the apostle Paul, the most energetic and influential spokesman for the new movement. Paul was a Hebrew zealot, a religious leader. His birth in Tarsus gave him exposure to the most advanced learning of his day. Tarsus was a university city known for its Stoic philosophers and culture. Strabo, the Greek geographer, praised Tarsus for its avid interest in education and philosophy.[1]

Paul, like his father, possessed Roman citizenship, a high privilege. Paul seemed to be well versed in Hellenistic culture and thought. He had great command of the Greek language and displayed superb dialectic skill. He often quoted from less familiar poets and philosophers. In one of his sermons Paul quotes and alludes to Epimenides, Aratus, and Cleanthes: "In him we live and move and exist. As some of your own poets have said, 'We are his offspring' " (Acts 17:28). In a letter Paul quotes Menander: "Don't be fooled by those who say such things, for 'bad company corrupts good character' " (1 Corinthians 15:33). In a later letter to Titus, Paul again quotes Epimenides: "One of their

> **What Do You Think?**
>
> *The apostle Paul completely reversed his beliefs about Jesus after experiencing a life-transforming encounter with him. Have you ever seen that kind of transformation in anyone? Have you ever experienced it?*

own men, a prophet from Crete, has said about them, 'The people of Crete are all liars, cruel animals, and lazy gluttons' " (Titus 1:12).

Paul's education was Jewish and took place under the strict doctrines of the Pharisees. When Paul was about age fourteen, he was sent to study under Gamaliel, the grandson of Hillel and one of the great rabbis of the time. Paul asserted that he was not only a Pharisee but also the son of Pharisees (see Acts 23:6). He could boast: "I was far ahead of my fellow Jews in my zeal for the traditions of my ancestors" (Galatians 1:14).

To understand Paul's conversion, it is necessary to see why he was so vehemently anti-Christian. It was his devotion to the Jewish law that triggered his adamant opposition to Christ and the early church. Paul's "offense with the Christian message was not," as French theologian Jacques Dupont writes,

> with the affirmation of Jesus' messiahship [but] . . . with the attributing to Jesus of a saving role which robbed the law of all its value in the purpose of salvation. . . . [Paul was] violently hostile to the Christian faith because of the importance which he attached to the law as a way of salvation.[2]

The *Encyclopaedia Britannica* states that the members of the new sect of Judaism calling themselves Christians struck at the essence of Paul's Jewish training and rabbinic studies.[3] He became passionate about exterminating this sect (see Galatians 1:13). So Paul began his pursuit to death of all Christians (see Acts 26:9-11). He single-mindedly began to destroy the church (see Acts 8:3). He set out for

Damascus with documents authorizing him to seize the followers of Jesus and bring them back to face trial.

Then something happened to Paul.

Meanwhile, Saul [later known as Paul] was uttering threats with every breath and was eager to destroy the Lord's followers. So he went to the high priest. He requested letters addressed to the synagogues in Damascus, asking for their cooperation in the arrest of any followers of the Way he found there. He wanted to bring them—both men and women—back to Jerusalem in chains.

The members of the new sect of Judaism calling themselves Christians struck at the essence of Paul's Jewish training and rabbinic studies. He became passionate about exterminating this sect.

As he was approaching Damascus on this mission, a light from heaven suddenly shone down around him. He fell to the ground and heard a voice saying to him, "Saul! Saul! Why are you persecuting me?"

"Who are you, lord?" Saul asked.

And the voice replied, "I am Jesus, the one you are persecuting! Now get up and go into the city, and you will be told what you must do."

The men with Saul stood speechless, for they heard the sound of someone's voice but saw no one! Saul picked himself up off the ground, but when he opened his eyes he was blind. So his companions led him by the hand to Damascus. He remained there blind for three days and did not eat or drink.

Now there was a believer in Damascus named Ananias. The Lord spoke to him in a vision, calling, "Ananias!"

"Yes, Lord!" he replied.

The Lord said, "Go over to Straight Street, to the house of Judas. When you get there, ask for a man from Tarsus named Saul. He is praying to me right now. I have shown him a vision of a man named Ananias coming in and laying his hands on him so he can see again." ACTS 9:1-12

As we read on, we can see why Christians feared Paul.

"But Lord," exclaimed Ananias, "I've heard many people talk about the terrible things this man has done to the believers in Jerusalem! And he is authorized by the leading priests to arrest everyone who calls upon your name."

But the Lord said, "Go, for Saul is my chosen instrument to take my message to the Gentiles and to kings, as well as to the people of Israel. And I will show him how much he must suffer for my name's sake."

So Ananias went and found Saul. He laid his hands on him and said, "Brother Saul, the Lord Jesus, who appeared to you on the road, has sent me so that you might regain your sight and be filled with the Holy Spirit." Instantly something like scales fell from Saul's eyes, and he regained his sight. Then he got up and was baptized. Afterward he ate some food and regained his strength.   ACTS 9:13-19

As a result of this experience, Paul considered himself a witness to the resurrected Christ. He later wrote, "Haven't I seen Jesus our Lord with my own eyes?" (1 Corinthians 9:1). He compared Christ's appearance to him with Christ's post-resurrection appearances to the other apostles. "Last of all, . . . I also saw him" (1 Corinthians 15:8).

What Do You Think?

Why do you think Paul's conversion had to be so dramatic? How did God's plan for Paul's life differ from Paul's plan for his life?

Not only did Paul see Jesus, but he saw him in an irresistible way. He didn't proclaim the gospel out of choice but from necessity. "Yet preaching the Good News is not something I can boast about. I am compelled by God to do it" (1 Corinthians 9:16).

Notice that Paul's encounter with Jesus and his subsequent conversion were sudden and unexpected: "a very bright light from heaven suddenly shone down around me" (Acts 22:6). He had no idea who this heavenly person could be. When the voice announced that he was Jesus of Nazareth, Paul was astonished and began to tremble.

We might not know all the details or psychology of what happened to Paul on the road to Damascus, but we do know this: The experience utterly overturned every area of his life.

First, Paul's character was radically transformed. The *Encyclopaedia Britannica* describes him before his conversion as an intolerant, bitter, persecuting, religious bigot—proud and temperamental. After his conversion it pictures him as patient, kind, enduring, and self-sacrificing.[4] Kenneth Scott Latourette says, "What integrated Paul's life, however, and lifted this almost neurotic temperament out of obscurity into enduring influence was a profound and revolutionary religious experience."[5]

Second, Paul's relationship with the followers of Jesus was transformed. They were no longer afraid of him. Paul "stayed with the believers in Damascus for a few days" (Acts 9:19). And when he went to meet the other apostles, they accepted him (Acts 9:27-28).

Third, Paul's message was transformed. Though he still loved his Jewish heritage, he had changed from a bitter antagonist to a determined protagonist of the Christian faith. "Immediately he began preaching about Jesus in the synagogues, saying, 'He is indeed the Son of God!' " (Acts 9:20). His intellectual convictions had changed. His experience compelled him to acknowledge that Jesus was the Messiah, in direct conflict with the Pharisees' messianic ideas. His new perspective of Christ meant a total revolution in his thinking.[6] Jacques Dupont acutely observes that after Paul "had passionately denied that a crucified man could be the Messiah, he came to grant that Jesus was indeed the Messiah, and, as a consequence, rethought all his messianic ideas."[7]

We might not know all the details or psychology of what happened to Paul on the road to Damascus, but we do know this: The experience utterly overturned every area of his life.

Also, Paul could now understand that Christ's death on the cross, which appeared to be a curse of God and a deplorable ending to a life, was actually God reconciling the world to himself through Christ. Paul came to understand that through the Crucifixion Christ took the curse of sin on himself for us (see Galatians 3:13) and that God "made Christ, who never sinned, to be the offering for our sin, so that we could be made right with God through Christ" (2 Corinthians 5:21). Instead of seeing the death of Christ as a defeat, he saw it as a great victory, completed by the Resurrection. The Cross was no longer a stumbling block but the essence of God's messianic redemption. Paul's missionary preaching can be summarized as "he explained the prophecies and proved that the Messiah must suffer and rise from the dead. He said, 'This Jesus I'm telling you about is the Messiah' " (Acts 17:3).

Instead of seeing the death of Christ as a defeat, Paul saw it as a great victory, completed by the Resurrection. The Cross was the essence of God's messianic redemption.

Fourth, Paul's mission was transformed. He was changed from a hater of the Gentiles to a missionary to the Gentiles. He was changed from a Jewish zealot to an evangelist to non-Jews. As a Jew and a Pharisee, Paul looked down on the despised Gentiles as inferior to God's chosen people. The Damascus experience changed him into a dedicated apostle with his life's mission aimed toward helping the Gentiles. Paul saw that the Christ who appeared to him was indeed the Savior for all people. Paul went from being an orthodox Pharisee, whose mission was to preserve strict Judaism, to being a propagator of that new, radical sect called Christianity, which he had so violently opposed. The change in him was so profound that "all who heard him were amazed. 'Isn't this the same man who caused such devastation among Jesus' followers in Jerusalem?' they asked. 'And didn't he come here to arrest them and take them in chains to the leading priests?' Saul's preaching became more and more powerful, and the Jews in Damascus couldn't refute his proofs that Jesus was indeed the Messiah" (Acts 9:21-22).

Historian Philip Schaff states:

> The conversion of Paul marks not only a turning-point in his personal history, but also an important epoch in the history of the apostolic church, and consequently in the history of mankind. It was the most fruitful event since the miracle of Pentecost, and secured the universal victory of Christianity.[8]

During lunch one day at the University of Houston, I sat down next to a student. As we discussed Christianity, he made the statement that there was no historical evidence for Christianity or Christ. I asked him why he thought that. He was a history major, and one of his textbooks was a Roman history text that contained a chapter dealing with the apostle Paul and Christianity. The student had read the chapter and found that it started by describing the life of Saul of Tarsus and ended describing the life of Paul the apostle. The book stated that what caused the change was not clear. I turned to the book of Acts and explained

Christ's post-resurrection appearance to Paul. The student saw immediately that this was the most logical explanation for Paul's radical conversion. This bit of missing evidence made the pieces fall into place for this young man. Later he became a Christian.

Elias Andrews, former principal of Queens Theological College, comments:

> Many have found in the radical transformation of this 'Pharisee of the Pharisees' the most convincing evidence of the truth and the power of the religion to which he was converted, as well as the ultimate worth and place of the Person of Christ.[9]

Archibald McBride, who was a professor at the University of Aberdeen, writes of Paul: "Beside his achievements . . . the achievements of Alexander and Napoleon pale into insignificance."[10] Early Christian scholar Clement of Alexandria says that Paul "bore chains seven times; preached the gospel in the East and West; came to the limit of the West; and died a martyr under the rulers."[11]

Paul states again and again that the living, resurrected Jesus had transformed his life. He was so convinced of Christ's resurrection from the dead that he, too, died a martyr's death for his beliefs.

What Do You Think?

In his day, Paul had celebrity status—people knew who he was. Today, when a celebrity becomes a Christian what is the initial reaction of most people? Should high-profile Christians be held to a different standard?

Two Oxford-educated friends, author Gilbert West and statesman Lord George Lyttleton, were determined to destroy the basis of the Christian faith. West was going to demonstrate the fallacy of the Resurrection, and Lyttleton was going to prove that Saul of Tarsus never converted to Christianity. Both men came to a complete turnaround in their positions and became ardent followers of Jesus. Lord Lyttleton writes: "The conversion and apostleship of Saint Paul alone, duly considered, was of itself a demonstration sufficient to prove Christianity to be a Divine Revelation."[12] He concludes that if Paul's twenty-five years of suffering and service for Christ were a reality, then his conversion was true, for everything he did began with that sudden change. And if Paul's conversion was true, then Jesus Christ rose from the dead, for everything Paul was and did he attributed to his witnessing the risen Christ.

CHAPTER 10

Can You Keep a Good Man Down?

A STUDENT AT THE UNIVERSITY OF URUGUAY ASKED ME, "Professor McDowell, why couldn't you find some way to refute Christianity?"

I answered, "For a very simple reason. I was unable to explain away the fact that the resurrection of Jesus Christ was a real event in history."

After spending more than seven hundred hours studying this subject and thoroughly investigating its foundation, I came to the conclusion that the resurrection of Jesus Christ is either one of the most wicked, vicious, heartless hoaxes ever foisted on humanity, or it is the most important fact in history.

The Resurrection takes the question "Is Christianity valid?" out of the realm of philosophy and makes it a question of history. Does Christianity have a solid historical basis? Is sufficient evidence available to warrant belief in the Resurrection?

Here are some of the issues and claims relevant to the

question: Jesus of Nazareth, a Jewish prophet who claimed to be the Christ prophesied in the Jewish Scriptures, was arrested, judged to be a political criminal, and crucified.

> **The resurrection of Jesus Christ is either one of the most wicked, vicious, heartless hoaxes ever foisted on humanity, or it is the most important fact in history.**

Three days after his death and burial, some women who went to his tomb found the body to be missing. Christ's disciples claimed that God had raised him from the dead and that he had appeared to them many times before ascending to heaven.

From this foundation, Christianity spread throughout the Roman Empire and has continued to exert great influence throughout the world through all subsequent centuries.

The big question is, Did the Resurrection actually happen?

The Death and Burial of Jesus

After Jesus was condemned to death, he was stripped of his clothing and was whipped, according to Roman custom, before crucifixion.

Alexander Metherell, who holds a medical degree from the University of Miami and a doctorate in engineering from the University of Bristol in England, made a detailed examination of Christ's whipping at the hands of the Romans. He explains the process:

> The soldier would use a whip of braided leather thongs with metal balls woven into them. When the

whip would strike the flesh, these balls would cause deep bruises or contusions, which would break open with further blows. And the whip had pieces of sharp bone as well, which would cut the flesh severely.

The back would be so shredded that part of the spine was sometimes exposed by the deep, deep cuts. The whipping would have gone all the way from the shoulders down to the back, the buttocks, and the back of the legs. It was just terrible.

One physician who has studied Roman beatings said, "As the flogging continued, the lacerations would tear into the underlying skeletal muscles and produce quivering ribbons of bleeding flesh." A third-century historian by the name of Eusebius described flogging by saying, "The sufferer's veins were laid bare, and the very muscles, sinews, and bowels of the victim were open to exposure."

We know that many people would die from this kind of beating even before they could be crucified. At the least, the victim would experience tremendous pain and go into hypovolemic shock.[1]

Given the brutality of the whipping, as well as his subsequent crucifixion, it is historically certain that Jesus was dead. Even the members of the radical Jesus Seminar, which was popular in the 1990s, accepted the death of Jesus. This is why John Dominic Crossan said that the death of Jesus by crucifixion "is as sure as anything historical can ever be."[2]

In accordance with Jewish burial customs, the body of Jesus was then wrapped in a linen cloth. About seventy-five pounds of aromatic spices, mixed together to form a gummy substance, were applied to the wrappings around the body (see John 19:39-40). After the body was placed in a solid rock tomb, an extremely large stone, weighing approximately two tons, was rolled by means of levers against the entrance (see Matthew 27:60).

What Do You Think?

Have you ever seen any movies about Jesus' life that included his death and resurrection, such as The Passion of the Christ? What went through your mind when you saw the torture and crucifixion of Christ? Do you think he deserved what happened to him?

A Roman guard of strictly disciplined men was stationed to watch the tomb. Fear of punishment among these men "produced flawless attention to duty, especially in the night watches."[3] This guard affixed on the tomb the Roman seal, a stamp of Roman power and authority.[4] The seal was meant to prevent vandalizing. Anyone trying to move the stone from the tomb's entrance would have broken the seal and thus incurred the wrath of Roman law.

Yet in spite of the guard and the seal, the tomb was empty.

The Empty Tomb

The followers of Jesus claimed he had risen from the dead. They reported that he appeared to them over a period of forty days, showing himself to them by many convincing proofs (some versions of the Bible say "infallible proofs"; see, for example, Acts 1:3, NKJV). The apostle Paul said that Jesus appeared to more than five hundred of his followers at one time, the majority of whom were still alive and could confirm what he wrote (see 1 Corinthians 15:3-8).

Arthur Michael Ramsey, former archbishop of Canterbury, writes: "I believe in the Resurrection, partly because a series of facts are unaccountable without it."[5] The empty tomb was "too notorious to be denied."[6] German theologian Paul Althaus states that the claim of the Resurrection "could not have been maintained in Jerusalem for a single day, for a single hour, if the emptiness of the tomb had not been established as a fact for all concerned."[7]

Paul L. Maier concludes:

> If all the evidence is weighed carefully and fairly, it is indeed justifiable, according to the canons of historical research, to conclude that [Jesus' tomb] was actually empty. . . . And no shred of evidence has yet been discovered in literary sources, epigraphy, or archaeology that would disprove this statement.[8]

How can we explain the empty tomb?

Based on overwhelming historical evidence, Christians believe that Jesus was bodily resurrected in real time and space by the supernatural power of God. The difficulties in belief may be great, but the problems inherent in disbelief are even greater.

The situation at the tomb after the Resurrection is

significant. The Roman seal was broken, which meant automatic crucifixion upside down for whoever broke it. The massive stone was moved not just from the entrance but from the entire sepulcher, looking as if it had been picked up and carried away.[9] The guard unit had fled. Byzantine Roman emperor Justinian in his Digest 49:16 lists eighteen offenses for which a Roman guard unit could be put to death. These included falling asleep or leaving one's position unguarded.

What Do You Think?

Have you ever been part of a group and something happened that involved all of you? Were your stories the same? How difficult is it to get everyone to tell the exact same story?

The women came and found the tomb empty. They panicked and went back to tell the men. Peter and John ran to the tomb. John arrived first, but he didn't enter. He looked inside and saw the graveclothes, caved in a little, but empty. The body of Christ had passed right through them into a new existence. Let's face it; a sight like that would make anyone a believer.

Alternative Theories to the Resurrection

Many people have advanced alternate theories to explain the Resurrection, but the theories are so contrived and illogical when compared with the claims of Christianity that their very weakness actually helps build confidence in the truth of the Resurrection.

The Wrong-Tomb Theory

A theory propounded by British biblical scholar Kirsopp Lake assumes that the women who reported the body missing had mistakenly gone to the wrong tomb that morning. If so, then the disciples who went to check the women's story must have gone to the wrong tomb as well. We can be certain, however, that the Jewish authorities, who had asked for that Roman guard to be stationed at the tomb to prevent the body from being stolen, would not have been mistaken about the location. The Roman guards would also not have been mistaken, for they were there. If a wrong tomb were involved, the Jewish authorities would have lost no time in producing the body from the proper tomb, thus effectively quenching for all time any rumor of a resurrection.

> **Based on historical evidence, Christians believe that Jesus was bodily resurrected in real time and space by the supernatural power of God. The difficulties in belief may be great, but the problems inherent in disbelief are even greater.**

The Hallucination Theory

Another attempted explanation claims that the appearances of Jesus after the Resurrection were either illusions or hallucinations. This theory runs counter to psychological principles governing the occurrence of hallucinations. It is not credible to think that five hundred people could have seen the same hallucination for forty days. Also the hallucination theory does not coincide with the historical situation or the mental state of the apostles.

So, where was the actual body of Jesus, and why didn't those who opposed him produce it?

The Swoon Theory

Nineteenth-century German rationalist Karl Venturini popularized the swoon theory several centuries ago, and it is often suggested even today. It claims that Jesus didn't really die; he merely fainted from exhaustion and loss of blood. Everyone thought he was dead, but later he was resuscitated, and the disciples thought it to be a resurrection.

German theologian David Friedrich Strauss, himself no believer in the Resurrection, deals a deathblow to any thought that Jesus could have revived from a swoon:

> It is impossible that a being who had stolen half-dead out of the sepulcher, who crept about weak and ill, wanting medical treatment, who required bandaging, strengthening and indulgence, and who still at last yielded to his sufferings, could have given to the disciples the impression that he was a Conqueror over death and the grave, the Prince of Life, an impression which lay at the bottom of their future ministry. Such a resuscitation could only have weakened the impression which He had made upon them in life and in death, at the most could only have given it an elegiac voice, but could by no possibility have changed their sorrow into enthusiasm, have elevated their reverence into worship.[10]

The Stolen-Body Theory

Another theory maintains that the disciples stole the body of Jesus while the guards slept. The depression and cowardice of the disciples make a hard-hitting argument against it. Can we imagine that they suddenly became so brave and daring as to face a detachment of select soldiers at the tomb and steal the body? They were in no mood to attempt anything like that.

Commenting on the proposition that the disciples stole Christ's body, J. N. D. Anderson says:

> This would run totally contrary to all we know of them: their ethical teaching, the quality of their lives, their steadfastness in suffering and persecution. Nor would it begin to explain their dramatic transformation from dejected and dispirited escapists into witnesses whom no opposition could muzzle.[11]

The Moved-Body Theory

Another theory says that the Roman or Jewish authorities moved Christ's body from the tomb. This explanation is no more reasonable than the stolen-body theory. If the authorities had the body in their possession or knew where it was, why didn't they explain that they had taken it, thus putting to an effective end the disciples' preaching of the Resurrection in Jerusalem? If the authorities had taken the body, why didn't they explain exactly where they had put it? Why didn't they recover the corpse, display it on a cart, and wheel it through the

If the authorities had taken the body, why didn't they display it on a cart, and wheel it through the center of Jerusalem? That action would have utterly destroyed Christianity.

center of Jerusalem? Such an action would have utterly destroyed Christianity.

John Warwick Montgomery comments:

> It passes the bounds of credibility that the early Christians could have manufactured such a tale and then preached it among those who might easily have refuted it simply by producing the body of Jesus.[12]

The Relocated-Body Theory

In *The Empty Tomb*, Jeffrey Jay Lowder describes an interesting hypothesis, namely, that the body of Jesus was temporarily stored in the tomb of Joseph of Arimathea on Friday night before being relocated to a criminal's tomb.[13] The tomb of Jesus was empty not because he resurrected, but because the body was simply relocated. Thus, the disciples mistakenly believed he was resurrected. This hypothesis has gained a considerable following on the Internet.

The "relocation hypothesis" gains support from the fact that reburial was common in ancient Palestine. But it's important to note that the reburial procedures of the Jews differed significantly from the theory proposed here. The Jewish tradition was to bury a body for one year, and then after the flesh deteriorated and only bones remained, they would remove the bones and place them in an ossuary.

The problem for the relocation of the body of Jesus is the complete lack of historical support, either in biblical or non-biblical sources. None of the New Testament Gospel accounts suggest that the body of Jesus was reburied. Mark 16:6, where the young man at the tomb says, "He isn't here! He is risen from the dead!" undermines this view.

The relocation hypothesis actually faces a more significant problem. Dr. Michael Licona observes

> At best, even if the reburial hypothesis were true, all it accounts for is the empty tomb. And interestingly, the empty tomb didn't convince any of the disciples—possibly with the exception of John—that Jesus had returned from the dead. It was the appearances of Jesus that convinced them, and the reburial theory can't account for these.[14]

If the body of Jesus was simply relocated, why didn't a relative uncover the body when the disciples began proclaiming the resurrection? Why wouldn't an authority produce the body and stop Christianity in its tracks? Some have suggested that by this time the body of Jesus would be unrecognizable, but given the climate of Palestine, the body would have been recognizable for a considerable amount of time.[15]

The Copycat Theory

"Nothing in Christianity is original" is one of the most commonly used lines of many critics today. In the late nineteenth and early twentieth centuries many scholars believed that the central claims of Christianity were plagiarized from Greco-Roman mystery religions. Jesus was considered another "dying and rising" god

What Do You Think?
Can you think of any other possible naturalistic explanations for Jesus' resurrection? Does any other theory explain as many facts surrounding the events as his actual resurrection?

in the tradition of Osiris, Mithras, Adonis, and Dionysus. While this theory has experienced a surprising resurgence on the Internet and in popular books, it faces near universal rejection by contemporary scholars. Here's why.

While parallels between Jesus and the mystery religions may appear striking on the surface, they collapse under scrutiny. Osiris, for instance, is considered by many to be a dying and rising god from ancient Egypt. According to the myth, Osiris was killed by Seth and resuscitated by Isis. But rather than returning to the world in a resurrected body, Osiris became king of the underworld—hardly a parallel to the historical resurrection of Jesus. This is why Paul Rhodes Eddy and Greg Boyd, authors of *The Jesus Legend*, conclude that "the differences between Christianity and the mystery religions are far more profound than any similarities. While there certainly are parallel terms used in early Christianity and the mystery religions, there is little evidence for parallel concepts."[16]

Unlike the historical Jesus, there is no evidence for the reliability of any of the alleged parallel stories in the mystery religions. Jesus of Nazareth ate, slept, performed miracles, died, and returned to life. These accounts are supported by a reliable historical record. In contrast, the dying and rising gods of the mystery religions were timeless myths repeated annually with the changing seasons.

The most recent scholarly treatise on dying and rising gods was written by T. N. D. Mettinger, professor at Lund University. In *The Riddle of Resurrection*, Mettinger grants the existence of the myths of dying and rising gods in the ancient world, which, he admits, is a minority view. Yet his conclusion puts the nail in the coffin of the copycat theory:

There is, as far as I am aware, no prima facie evidence that the death and resurrection of Jesus is a mythological construct, drawing on the myths and rites of the dying and rising gods of the surrounding world. While studied with profit against the background of Jewish resurrection belief, the faith in the death and resurrection of Jesus retains its unique character in the history of religions. The riddle remains.[17]

Evidence for the Resurrection

Professor Thomas Arnold, author of a famous three-volume *History of Rome* and the chair of modern history at Oxford, was well acquainted with the value of evidence in determining historical facts. He says:

I have been used for many years to study the histories of other times, and to examine and weigh the evidence of those who have written about them, and I know of no one fact in the history of mankind which is proved by better and fuller evidence of every sort, to the understanding of a fair inquirer, than the great sign which God has given us that Christ died and rose again from the dead.[18]

British scholar Brooke Foss Westcott, who was a divinity professor at Cambridge University, says:

Taking all the evidence together, it is not too much to say that there is no historic incident better or more variously supported than the resurrection of Christ. Nothing but the antecedent assumption that it must be false could have suggested the idea of deficiency in the proof of it.[19]

Dr. William Lane Craig concludes that "when you . . . [use] the ordinary canons of historical assessment, the best explanation for the facts is that God raised Jesus from the dead."[20]

Simon Greenleaf was one of the greatest legal minds America has produced. He was the famous Royall Professor of Law at Harvard University and succeeded Justice Joseph Story as the Dane Professor of Law in the same university. While at Harvard, Greenleaf wrote a volume in which he examines the legal value of the apostles' testimony to the resurrection of Christ. He observes that it is impossible that the apostles "could have persisted in affirming the truths they had narrated, had not Jesus actually risen from the dead, and had they not known this fact as certainly as they knew any other fact."[21]

> **It is impossible that the apostles "could have persisted in affirming the truths they had narrated, had not Jesus actually risen from the dead."**

Greenleaf concludes that the resurrection of Christ is one of the best-supported events in history according to the laws of legal evidence administered in courts of justice.

Sir Lionel Luckhoo is considered by many to be the world's most successful attorney after 245 consecutive murder acquittals. This brilliant lawyer rigorously analyzed the historical facts of Christ's resurrection and finally declares, "I say unequivocally that the evidence for the resurrection of Jesus Christ is so overwhelming that it compels acceptance by proof which leaves absolutely no room for doubt."[22]

Frank Morison, another British lawyer, set out to refute the evidence for the Resurrection. He thought the life of Jesus was one of the most beautiful ever lived, but when it came to the Resurrection, Morison assumed someone had come along and tacked a myth onto the story. He planned to write an account of the last few days of Jesus, disregarding the Resurrection. The lawyer figured that an intelligent, rational approach to the story would completely discount such an event. However, when he applied his legal training to the facts, he had to change his mind. Instead of a refutation of the Resurrection, he eventually wrote the best seller *Who Moved the Stone?* He titled the first chapter "The Book That Refused to Be Written." The rest of the book confirms decisively the validity of the evidence for Christ's resurrection.[23]

George Eldon Ladd concludes: "The only rational explanation for these historical facts is that God raised Jesus in bodily form."[24] Believers in Jesus Christ today can have complete confidence, as did the first Christians, that their faith is based not on myth or legend but on the solid historical fact of the risen Christ and the empty tomb.

Gary Habermas, a distinguished professor and chairman of the department of philosophy and theology at Liberty University, debated former atheist and leading scholar Antony Flew on the issue "Did Jesus Rise from the Dead?" A professional debate judge who was asked to evaluate the debate concludes,

> The historical evidence, though flawed, is strong enough to lead reasonable minds to conclude that

Christ did indeed rise from the dead. . . . Habermas does end up providing "highly probably evidence" for the historicity of the resurrection "with no plausible naturalistic evidence against it."[25]

Most important of all, individual believers can experience the power of the risen Christ in their lives today. First of all, they can know that their sins are forgiven (see Luke 24:46-47; 1 Corinthians 15:3). Second, they can be assured of eternal life and their own resurrection from the grave (see 1 Corinthians 15:19-26). Third, they can be released from a meaningless and empty life and be transformed into new creatures in Jesus Christ (see John 10:10; 2 Corinthians 5:17).

What Do You Think?

Is the fact that Jesus rose from the dead 2,000 years ago relevant to you today? If so, how and why?

What is your evaluation and decision? What do you think about the empty tomb? After examining the evidence from a judicial perspective, Lord Darling, former chief justice of England, concludes that "there exists such overwhelming evidence, positive and negative, factual and circumstantial, that no intelligent jury in the world could fail to bring in a verdict that the resurrection story is true."[26]

CHAPTER 11

Will the Real Messiah Please Stand Up?

OF ALL THE CREDENTIALS JESUS HAD TO SUPPORT HIS claims to be the Messiah and God's Son, one of the most profound is often overlooked: how his life fulfilled so many ancient prophecies. In this chapter I will deal with this astounding fact.

Over and over Jesus appealed to Old Testament prophecies to substantiate his claims. Galatians 4:4 says, "But when the right time came, God sent his Son, born of a woman, subject to the law." Here we have reference to the prophecies being fulfilled in Jesus Christ. "Then Jesus took them through the writings of Moses and all the prophets, explaining from all the Scriptures the things concerning himself" (Luke 24:27). Jesus said to them, "When I was with you before, I told you that everything written about me in the law of Moses and the prophets and in the Psalms must be fulfilled" (Luke 24:44). He said, "If you really believed Moses, you would believe me, because he wrote about me" (John 5:46). He said, "Your father Abraham rejoiced as he looked forward to my coming" (John 8:56).

The apostles and the New Testament writers also constantly appealed to fulfilled prophecy to substantiate the claims of Jesus as the Son of God, the Savior, and the Messiah. "God was fulfilling what all the prophets had foretold about the Messiah—that he must suffer these things" (Acts 3:18). "As was Paul's custom, he went to the synagogue service, and for three Sabbaths in a row he used the Scriptures to reason with the people. He was explained the prophecies and proved that the Messiah must suffer and rise from the dead. He said, 'This Jesus I'm telling you about is the Messiah'" (Acts 17:2-3). "I passed on to you what was most important and what had also been passed on to me. Christ died for our sins, just as the Scriptures said. He was buried, and he was raised from the dead on the third day, as the Scriptures said" (1 Corinthians 15:3-4).

> **What Do You Think?**
>
> *Do you think there is any difference between a prophecy and a prediction? Has anything ever been predicted about you at an early age that came true later? How is that different from the prophecies that Jesus fulfilled?*

The Old Testament contains sixty major messianic prophecies and approximately 270 ramifications that were fulfilled in one person, Jesus Christ. It is helpful to look at all these predictions fulfilled in Christ as his "address." Let me explain. You've probably never realized the importance of your own name and address, yet these details set you apart from the more than six billion other people who also inhabit this planet.

An Address in History

With even greater detail, God wrote an "address" in history to single out his Son, the Messiah, the Savior of humanity, from anyone who has ever lived in history—past, present, or future. The specifics of this address can be found in the Old Testament, a document that was written over a period of a thousand years and that contains more than three hundred references to Christ's coming. Using the science of probability, we find the chances of just forty-eight of these prophecies being fulfilled in one person to be only 1 in 10^{157}.

The likelihood of God's address matching up with one man is further complicated by the fact that all of the prophecies about the Messiah were made at least four hundred years before he was to appear. Some might suggest that these prophecies were written down after the time of Christ and fabricated to coincide with events in his life. This might seem possible until you realize that the Septuagint, the Greek translation of the Hebrew Old Testament, was translated around 150–200 BC. This means that there is at least a two-hundred-year gap between the recording of the prophecies and their fulfillment in Christ.

Certainly God was writing an address in history that only his Messiah could fulfill. Approximately forty men have claimed to be the Jewish Messiah. But only one—Jesus Christ—appealed to fulfilled prophecy to substantiate his claims, and only his credentials back up those claims.

What are some of those credentials? And what events had to precede and coincide with the appearance of God's Son?

To begin, we must go back to Genesis 3:15, where we

find the first messianic prophecy in the Bible: "I will put enmity between you and the woman, and between your seed and her Seed; He shall bruise your head, and you shall bruise His heel" (NKJV). This prophecy could refer to only one man in all of Scripture. No other but Jesus could be referred to as the "seed" of a woman. All others born in history come from the seed of a man. Other versions make the same claim when they identify this conqueror of Satan to be the offspring of a woman, when in all other instances the Bible counts offspring through the line of the man. This offspring or "seed" of a woman will come into the world and destroy the works of Satan (bruise his head).

In Genesis 9 and 10 God narrowed down the address further. Noah had three sons: Shem, Ham, and Japheth. All the nations of the world can be traced back to these three men. But God effectively eliminated two-thirds of the human race from the line of messiahship by specifying that the Messiah would come through the lineage of Shem.

Then continuing on down to the year 2000 BC, we find that God called a man named Abraham out of Ur of the Chaldees. With Abraham, God became still more specific, stating that the Messiah will be one of his descendants. All the families of the earth will be blessed through Abraham (see Genesis 12:1-3; 17:1-8; 22:15-18). When he had two sons, Isaac and Ishmael, many of Abraham's descendants were eliminated when God selected the second son, Isaac, to be the progenitor of the Messiah (see Genesis 17:19-21; 21:12).

Isaac had two sons, Jacob and Esau. God chose the line of Jacob (see Genesis 28:1-4; 35:10-12; Numbers 24:17). Jacob had twelve sons, out of whose descendants developed the twelve tribes of Israel. Then God singled out the tribe of

Judah for messiahship and eliminated eleven-twelfths of the Israelite tribes. And of all the family lines within the tribe of Judah, he chose the line of Jesse (see Isaiah 11:1-5, NIV). We can see the address narrowing.

Jesse had eight sons, and in 2 Samuel 7:12-16 and Jeremiah 23:5 God eliminated seven-eighths of Jesse's family line by choosing Jesse's son David. So, in terms of lineage, the Messiah must be born of the seed of a woman, the lineage of Shem, the race of the Jews, the line of Isaac, the line of Jacob, the tribe of Judah, the family of Jesse, and the house of David.

In Micah 5:2 God eliminated all the cities of the world and selected Bethlehem, with a population of less than one thousand people, as the Messiah's birthplace.

> **What Do You Think?**
> *Have you ever explored your ancestry? Did you discover any interesting information about your family? Do you know anything about Jesus' ancestry? What do you find the most interesting about it?*

Then through a series of prophecies he even defined the time period that would set this man apart. For example, Malachi 3:1 and four other Old Testament verses require the Messiah to come while the Temple of Jerusalem is still standing (see Psalm 118:26; Daniel 9:26; Zechariah 11:13; Haggai 2:7-9).[1] This is of great significance when we realize that the Temple was destroyed in AD 70 and has not since been rebuilt.

Isaiah 7:14 adds that Christ will be born of a virgin. A natural birth of unnatural conception was a criterion beyond human planning and control. Several prophecies recorded in Isaiah and the Psalms describe the social climate and response that God's man will encounter: His own people, the Jews, will reject him, and the Gentiles will believe in him (see Psalms 22:7-8; 118:22; Isaiah 8:14; 49:6; 50:6; 52:13-15). He will have a forerunner, a voice in the wilderness, one preparing the way before the Lord, a John the Baptist (see Isaiah 40:3-5; Malachi 3:1).

Notice how one passage in the New Testament (Matthew 27:3-10) refers to certain Old Testament prophecies that narrow down Christ's address even further. Matthew describes the events brought about by the actions of Judas after he betrayed Jesus. Matthew points out that these events were predicted in passages from the Old Testament (see Psalm 41:9; Zechariah 11:12-13).[2] In these passages God indicates that the Messiah will (1) be betrayed, (2) by a friend, (3) for thirty pieces of silver, and that the money will be (4) cast on the floor of the Temple. Thus the address becomes even more specific.

> The precise lineage; the place, time, and manner of birth; the manner of death—a fraction of the hundreds of details that make up the "address" to identify God's Son, the Savior of the world.

A prophecy dating from 1012 BC also predicts that this man's hands and feet will be pierced and that he will be crucified (see Psalm 22:6-18; Zechariah 12:10; Galatians 3:13). This description of the manner of his death was written eight hundred years before the Romans used crucifixion as a method of execution.

The precise lineage; the place, time, and manner of birth; people's reactions; the betrayal; the manner of death—these are merely a fraction of the hundreds of details that make up the "address" to identify God's Son, the Messiah, the Savior of the world.

Were These Fulfilled Prophecies Coincidental?

A critic could claim, "Why, you could find some of these prophecies fulfilled in Abraham Lincoln, Anwar Sadat, John F. Kennedy, Mother Teresa, or Billy Graham."

Yes, I suppose one could possibly find one or two prophecies coincident to other people, but not all sixty major prophecies and 270 ramifications. In fact, for years, the Christian Victory Publishing Company of Denver offered a one-thousand-dollar reward to anyone who could find any person other than Jesus, either living or dead, who could fulfill only half of the messianic predictions outlined in the book *Messiah in Both Testaments* by Fred John Meldau. They got no takers.

Could one person fulfill all of the Old Testament prophecies? In their book *Science Speaks*, Peter Stoner and Robert Newman did calculations to analyze that probability. Writing in the foreword to that book, H. Harold Hartzler of the American Scientific Affiliation says:

What Do You Think?
How likely do you think it is for one person to literally fulfill so many ancient predictions that were said hundreds of years before the person was born? How is it possible that Jesus did?

> The manuscript for *Science Speaks* has been carefully reviewed by a committee of the

American Scientific Affiliation members and by the Executive Council of the same group and has been found, in general, to be dependable and accurate in regard to the scientific material presented. The mathematical analysis included is based upon principles of probability which are thoroughly sound, and Professor Stoner has applied these principles in a proper and convincing way.[3]

The following probabilities show that coincidence is ruled out. Stoner says that by applying the science of probability to eight prophecies, "we find that the chance that any man might have lived down to the present time and fulfilled all eight prophecies is 1 in 10^{17} [10 to the 17th power]."[4] That is one in 100,000,000,000,000,000. To help us comprehend this staggering probability, Stoner illustrates it by supposing that

we take 10^{17} silver dollars and lay them on the face of Texas. They will cover all of the state two feet deep. Now mark one of these silver dollars and stir the whole mass thoroughly, all over the state. Blindfold a man and tell him that he can travel as far as he wishes, but he must pick up one silver dollar, and say that this is the right one. What chance would he have of getting the right one? Just the same chance that the prophets would have had of writing these eight prophecies and having them all come true in any one man, from their day to the present time, providing they wrote them in their own wisdom.

Now these prophecies were either given by inspiration of God or the prophets just wrote them as they thought they should be. In such a case the prophets had just one chance in 10^{17} of having them come true in any man, but they all came true in Christ.

This means that the fulfillment of these eight prophecies alone proves that God inspired the writing of those prophecies to a definiteness which lacks only one chance of 10^{17} of being absolute.[5]

Another Objection

Some claim that Jesus deliberately attempted to fulfill the Jewish prophecies. This objection seems plausible until we realize that many details of the Messiah's coming were totally beyond human control. One example is the place of his birth. When Herod asked the chief priests and scribes where the Christ was to be born, they replied, "In Bethlehem . . . for this is what the prophet wrote" (Matthew 2:5). It would be foolish to think that as Mary and Joseph traveled to the predicted town, Jesus, in his mother's womb, said, "Mom, you'd better hurry or we won't make it."

Half the prophecies were

Why did God go to all this trouble? I believe he wanted Jesus Christ to have all the credentials he needed when he came into the world. Yet one of the most exciting things about Jesus is that he came to change lives.

beyond Christ's control to fulfill: the manner of his birth; his betrayal by Judas and the betrayal price; the manner of his death; the people's reaction, the mocking and spitting, the staring; the casting of dice for his clothes and the soldiers' hesitance to tear his garment. Furthermore, Christ couldn't cause himself to be born of the seed of a woman, in the lineage of Shem, descending from Abraham, and all of the other events that led to his birth. It's no wonder Jesus and the apostles appealed to fulfilled prophecy to substantiate his claim that he was the Son of God.

Why did God go to all this trouble? I believe he wanted Jesus Christ to have all the credentials he needed when he came into the world. Yet one of the most exciting things about Jesus is that he came to change lives. He alone proved correct the hundreds of Old Testament prophecies that described his coming. And he alone can fulfill the greatest prophecy of all for those who will accept it—the promise of new life: "I will give you a new heart, and I will put a new spirit in you" (Ezekiel 36:26). "This means that anyone who belongs to Christ has become a new person. The old life is gone; a new life has begun!" (2 Corinthians 5:17).

What Do You Think?

Of the three key evidences offered in this book—the reliability of the Bible, the historical evidence for the Resurrection, and fulfilled prophecy—which do you find most convincing? Why?

CHAPTER 12

Isn't There Some Other Way?

During a lecture series at the University of Texas, a graduate student approached me and asked, "Why is Jesus the only way to a relationship with God?" I had shown that Jesus claimed to be the only way to God, that the testimony of the Scriptures and the apostles was reliable, and that there was sufficient evidence to warrant faith in Jesus as Savior and Lord. Yet the student still had questions: "Why Jesus only? Isn't there some other way to God?" Strangely, like this young man, people continually look for alternatives. "What about Buddha? Muhammad? Can't a person simply live a good life? If God is such a loving God, then won't he accept all people just the way they are?"

These questions are typical of what I often hear. In today's open climate, people seem offended by the exclusive claims that Jesus is the only way to God and the only source of forgiveness of sin and salvation. This attitude shows that many people simply don't understand the nature of God. We can see the core of their misunderstanding in the question they usually ask: "How can a loving God allow anyone to go to hell?" I often turn the question around and ask, "How can a holy, just, and righteous God allow a sinful person into his presence?" Most people understand God to be a loving God, but they don't go any further. He is not only a God of love but also a God who is righteous, just, and holy. He cannot tolerate sin in his heaven any more than you would tolerate a filthy, foul-smelling, diseased dog to live in your home. This misunderstanding about the basic nature and character of God is the cause of many theological and ethical problems.

What Do You Think?

How would you describe God? Where did your ideas of God originate? Is there anything about Jesus that surprises you, that doesn't seem to fit a description of God?

Basically, we know God through his attributes. However, his attributes are not parts of him in the same way that the attributes you have adopted are parts of you. You may realize it is good to be courteous and adopt this attribute as a part of your overall makeup. With God it works the other way around. God's attributes, his very being, include such qualities as holiness, love, justice, and righteousness. For example, goodness is not a part of God but rather something that is true of God's very nature. God's attributes have their source in who God is. He didn't adopt them to make up his nature; they flow from his nature. So when we say God is love, we don't mean that a part of God is love but that love is an attribute that is innately true of God. When God loves, he is not making a decision; he is simply being himself.

Here's the problem as it relates to us: If God's nature is love, how can he possibly send anyone to hell? The answer in a nutshell is that God doesn't send people to hell; they go because of their own choices. To explain, we must go all the way back to Creation. The Bible indicates that God created man and woman so he could share his love and glory with them. But Adam and Eve chose to rebel and go their own way. They left God's love and protection, contaminating themselves with that self-willed, grasping, prideful nature we call sin. Because God dearly loved the man and woman—even after they spurned him—he wanted to reach out to them and save them from the deadly path they had chosen. But God faced a dilemma. Because God is not only loving but also holy, righteous, and just, sin cannot survive in his presence. His very holy, just, and righteous nature would destroy the sinful couple. This is why the Bible says, "The wages of sin is death" (Romans 6:23). So how could God resolve this dilemma and save the man and woman?

We know God through his attributes—his holiness, love, justice, and righteousness. He didn't adopt these attributes; they flow from his nature.

The Godhead—God the Father, God the Son, and God the Holy Spirit—made an astounding decision. Jesus, God the Son, would take upon himself human flesh. He would become the God-man. We read of this in the first chapter of the Gospel of John, where it says that "the Word became flesh, and dwelt among us" (John 1:14, NASB). Also Philippians 2 tells us that Christ Jesus emptied himself of his godlike prerogatives and took on human form (see Philippians 2:6-7).

Jesus was the God-man. He was just as much man as if he had never been God and just as much God as if he had never been man. His humanity did not diminish his

What Do You Think?

Has anyone ever taken a punishment for you? Did your relationship with that person change after that? Would you be willing to do the same for that person, even if they deserved to be punished?

deity, and his deity did not overpower his humanity. By his own choice he lived a sinless life, wholly obeying the Father. The biblical declaration that "the wages of sin is death" did not indict him. Because he was not only finite man but also infinite God, he had the infinite capacity to take on himself the sins of the world. When Jesus was executed on the cross more than

two thousand years ago, God accepted his death as a substitute for ours. The just and righteous nature of God was satisfied. Justice was done; a penalty was paid. So at that point God's love nature was set free from the constrictions of justice, and he could accept us again and offer us what we had lost in Eden—that original relationship in which we could experience his love and glory.

Often I ask people, "For whom did Jesus die?" Usually they reply, "For me" or "For the world." And I will say, "Yes, that is right, but for whom else did Jesus die?" They generally admit that they don't know. I will reply, "For God the Father." You see, not only did Christ die for us, but he also died for the Father. This is addressed in the last section of Romans 3, where some versions of the Bible call the death of Jesus a "propitiation" (see Romans 3:25, NASB). *Propitiation* basically means the satisfaction of a requirement. When Jesus died on the cross, he died not only for us, but he also died to meet the holy and just requirements intrinsic in the basic nature of God. The contamination was removed so we could stand clean in his presence.

Jesus was just as much man as if he had never been God and just as much God as if he had never been man.

Several years ago I heard a true story that illuminates what Jesus did on the cross to solve God's problem in dealing with our sin. A young woman was stopped for speeding. The police officer ticketed her and took her before the judge. The judge read off the citation and asked, "Guilty or not guilty?" The woman replied, "Guilty." The judge brought down the gavel and fined her one hundred dollars or ten days in jail. Then he did an amazing thing. He stood up, took off his robe, stepped down from the bench, took out his billfold, and paid the young woman's fine. Why? The judge was her father. He loved his daughter, yet he was a just judge. She had broken the law, and he couldn't simply say to her,

What Do You Think?

Do you find it difficult to forgive someone who has wronged you? What price do most people pay when they forgive others?

"Because I love you so much, I forgive you. You may go scot-free." Had he done such a thing, he would not have been a righteous judge. He would not have upheld the law. But because of his love for his daughter, he was willing to take off his judicial robe, step down to her position, assume his relationship as her father, and pay the fine.

This story illustrates in a small way what God did for us through Jesus Christ. We sinned, and the Bible says that "the wages of sin is death." When God looks at us, in spite of his tremendous love for us, he has to bring down the gavel and say *death* because he is a righteous and just God. And yet, because he is also a loving God, he was willing to come down off his throne in the form of the man Jesus Christ and pay the price for us, which was his death on the cross.

Forgiveness always has a price. God paid the price for our forgiveness through the Cross—a payment that Buddha, Muhammad, Confucius, or any other religious leader cannot offer.

At this point many people ask the natural question, "Why couldn't God just forgive without requiring any payment?" An executive in a large corporation once told me, "My employees often damage equipment, waste materials, and break things, and I just forgive them. Are you telling me I can do something that God can't do?" The executive failed to realize that his forgiveness cost him something. His company paid for his employees' failures by repairing and replacing damaged items. Wherever there is forgiveness, there is payment. For example, let's say my daughter breaks a lamp in my home. I'm a loving and forgiving father, so I hug her and say, "Don't cry, honey. Daddy loves you and forgives you." Usually the person who hears that story will say, "That's exactly what God ought to do." Then comes the question, "Who pays for the lamp?" The fact is, *I* do. Forgiveness always has a price. Let's say someone insults you in front of others, and later you graciously say, "I forgive you." Who bears the price of that insult? You do. You bear the pain of the lie and the loss of reputation in the eyes of those who witnessed the insult.

This is what God has done for us: He has said, "I forgive you." But he paid the price for the forgiveness himself through the Cross. It's a payment that Buddha, Muhammad, Confucius, or any other religious or ethical leader cannot offer. No one can pay the price by "just living a good life." I know it sounds exclusive to say it, but we must say it simply because it is true: There is no other way but Jesus.

CHAPTER 13

He Changed
My Life

WHAT I HAVE SHARED WITH YOU IN THIS BOOK IS WHAT I learned after digging through the evidence for Christianity after my friends at the university challenged me to prove the truth of their claims. You would think that after examining the evidence, I would have immediately jumped on board and become a Christian. But in spite of the abundant evidence, I felt a strong reluctance to make the plunge. My mind was convinced of the truth. I had to admit that Jesus Christ must be exactly who he claimed to be. I could plainly see that Christianity was not a myth, not a fantasy of wishful dreamers, not a hoax played on the simple-minded, but rock-solid truth. I knew the truth, yet my will was pulling me in another direction.

There were two reasons for my reluctance: pleasure and pride. I thought that becoming a Christian meant giving up the good life and giving up control. I could sense Jesus Christ at the door of my heart, pleading, "Look, I have been standing at your door and constantly knocking. If you hear me calling and will open the door, I will come in" (paraphrased from Revelation 3:20). I kept that door shut and bolted. I didn't care if he did walk on water or turn water into wine. I didn't want any party pooper spoiling my fun. I couldn't think of any faster way to ruin my good times. I called them good times, but I was really miserable. I was a walking battlefield. My mind was telling me that Christianity was true, but my will was resisting it with all the energy it could muster.

Then there was the pride problem. At that time the thought of becoming a Christian shattered my ego. I had just proved that all my previous thinking had been wrong and my friends had been right. Every time I got around those enthusiastic Christians, the inner conflict would boil over. If you've ever been in the company of happy people when you are miserable, you know how their joy can get under your skin. Sometimes I would literally get up, leave the group, and run right out of the student union. It came to the point where I would go to bed at ten o'clock at night but wouldn't get to sleep until four in the morning. I couldn't let go of the problem. I had to do something before it drove me out of my mind.

My mind was telling me that Christianity was true, but my will was resisting it with all the energy it could muster.

I always tried to be open-minded, but not so open-minded that my brains would fall out. As G. K. Chesterton says, "The purpose of opening the mind, as of opening the mouth, is to close it again on something solid." I opened my mind, and I finally closed it on the most solid reality I had ever experienced. On December 19, 1959, at 8:30 p.m., during my second year at the university, I became a Christian.

Someone asked me, "How do you know you became a Christian?" One of several answers was simple: "It has changed my life." It is this transformation that assures me of the validity of my conversion. That night I prayed four things to establish a relationship with the resurrected, living Christ, and I am grateful that this prayer has been answered.

First, I said, "Lord Jesus, thank you for dying on the cross for me." Second, I said, "I confess those things in my life that aren't pleasing to you and ask you to forgive and cleanse me." God tells us that, "No matter how deep the stain of your sins, I can remove it. I can make you as clean as freshly fallen snow" (Isaiah 1:18, paraphrased). Third, I said, "Right now, in the best way I know how, I open the door of my heart and life and trust you as my Savior and Lord. Take control of my life. Change me from the inside out. Make me the type of person you created me to be." The last thing I prayed was, "Thank you for coming into my life by faith." It was a faith based not on ignorance but on evidence, the facts of history, and God's Word.

I'm sure you have heard people speak of the "bolt of lightning" that hit them when they had their first religious experience. Well, it wasn't that dramatic for me. After I prayed, nothing happened. I mean *nothing*. And I still

> **What Do You Think?**
> Now that you are at the end of the book, have any of your thoughts about Jesus Christ changed? Are you challenged to read more about him? To talk to others who have given their lives to him?

haven't sprouted wings or a halo. In fact, after I made that decision, I felt worse. I actually felt that I was about to vomit. *Oh no, what have I gotten sucked into now?* I wondered. I really felt I had gone off the deep end (and I'm sure some people think I did!).

How do I know I became a Christian? It has changed my life. My faith was based not on ignorance but on evidence, the facts of history, and God's Word.

The change was not immediate, but it was real. In six to eighteen months, I knew that I had not gone off the deep end. My life *was* changed. At about that time I was in a debate with the head of the history department at a Midwestern university. I was telling him about my new life, and he interrupted me with, "McDowell, are you trying to tell me that God has really changed your life? Give me some specifics." After listening to me explain for forty-five minutes, he finally said, "Okay, okay, that's enough!"

One change I told him about was relief from my restlessness. Before I accepted Christ, I always had to be occupied. I had to be over at my girlfriend's place, at a party, at the student union, or running around with friends. I'd walk across the campus with my mind in a whirlwind of conflicts. I was always bouncing off the walls. I'd sit down and try to study or cogitate but couldn't do it. But after I made that decision for Christ, a kind of mental peace settled over me. Don't misunderstand; I don't mean all conflicts ceased. What I found in this relationship with Jesus wasn't so much the absence of conflict as the ability to cope with it. I wouldn't trade that for anything in the world.

Another area that began to change was my bad temper. I used to blow my stack if anyone just looked at me cross-eyed. I still have the scars from a fight in which I almost killed a man my first year in the university. My temper was such a part of me that I didn't consciously seek to change it. But one day I encountered a crisis that should have set me off,

What Do You Think?
If there was one area of your life that you would like God to change, what would it be?

only to find that I stayed calm and collected. My temper was gone! It wasn't my doing; as I've been telling you, Jesus changed my life. That doesn't mean I was perfect. I went fourteen years without losing my temper, but when I did blow it, I'm afraid I made up for all those times I didn't.

Jesus changed me in another way. I'm not proud of it, but I mention it because many people need the same change, and I want to show them the source of that change: a relationship with the resurrected, living Christ. The problem is hatred. I had a heavy load of hatred weighing me down. It didn't show outwardly, but it kept grinding away inwardly. I was ticked off

What I found in this relationship with Jesus wasn't so much the absence of conflict as the ability to cope with it.

with people, with things, with issues. I was insecure. Every time I met anyone different from me, that person became a threat, and I reacted with some level of hatred.

I hated one man more than anyone else in the world—my father. I hated his guts. I was mortified that he was the town alcoholic. If you're from a small town and one of your parents is an alcoholic, you know what I mean. Everybody knows. My high school friends would make jokes about my father's drinking. They didn't think it bothered me because I fell in with the joking and laughed with them. I was laughing on the outside, but let me tell you, I was crying on the inside. I would go to the barn and find my mother beaten so badly she couldn't get up, lying in the manure behind the cows. When we had friends over, I would take my father out to the barn, tie him up, and park his car behind the silo. We would tell our guests he'd had to go somewhere. I don't think anyone could hate a person more than I hated my father.

About five months after I made that decision for Christ, a love from God entered my life so powerfully that it took that hatred, turned it upside down, and emptied it out. I was able to look my father squarely in the eyes and say, "Dad, I love you." And I really meant it. After some of the things I'd done to him, that really shook him up.

I hated one man more than anyone else in the world—my father. But God's love entered my life so powerfully that it emptied me of that hatred.

After I transferred to a private university, a serious car accident put me in the hospital. When I was moved home to recover, my father came to visit me. Remarkably, he was sober that day. But he seemed uneasy, pacing about the room. Then he blurted out, "Son, how can you love a father like me?" I answered, "Dad, six months ago I despised you." Then I shared with him the story of my research and conclusions about Jesus Christ. I told him, "I have placed my trust in Christ, received God's forgiveness, invited him into my life, and he has changed me. I can't explain it all, Dad, but God has taken away my hatred and replaced it with the capacity to love. I love you and accept you just the way you are."

We talked for almost an hour, and then I received one of the greatest thrills of my life. This man who was my father, this man who knew me too well for me to pull the wool over his eyes, looked at me and said, "Son, if God can do in my life what I've seen him do in yours, then I want to give him the opportunity. I want to trust him as my Savior and Lord." I cannot imagine a greater miracle.

Usually after a person accepts Christ, the changes in his or her life occur over a period of days, weeks, months, or even years. In my own life the change took about six to eighteen months. But the life of my father changed right before my eyes. It was as if God reached down and flipped on the light switch. Never before or since have I seen such a dramatic change. My father touched an alcoholic beverage only once after that day. He got it as far as his lips before thrusting it away. Forever. I can come to only one conclusion: a relationship with Jesus Christ changes lives.

What Do You Think?

Why is it difficult to separate the faith of Christianity from the man, Jesus Christ? Can you see how the two are often viewed as being in opposition?

There was another person in my life that I needed to forgive. His name was Wayne, a man who worked for my parents when I was growing up on the farm. When my mom had to run an errand or was gone for a longer period of time, Wayne was put in charge of watching me. Mom would march me up to Wayne and say, "Now you obey Wayne and do everything he asks you to do. If you don't, you are going to get a thrashing when I get home." Trust me; you didn't want to get a thrashing from my mother.

But I would have gladly taken the thrashings if I had known what Wayne had in store for me. From the time I was six years old until I was thirteen, he sexually abused me regularly. When I told my mother, she refused to believe me. At thirteen, I threatened Wayne. "If you ever touch me again, I will kill you." Wayne knew I was serious and he stopped.

I wanted Wayne to burn in hell and I was willing to escort him there. The memories of the abuse scarred me. But after coming to Christ I knew I needed to forgive Wayne, just as I had forgiven my father. I confronted Wayne once again and said, "Wayne, what you did to me was evil. But I've trusted Jesus Christ as Savior and Lord and have become a Christian. I've come to tell you that Jesus died as much for you as he did for me. I forgive you." It was one of the most difficult things I've ever had to do. I could never have done it on my own. If you have a similar story, be assured that you don't have to face your demons alone either. Your past *can* be overcome with God's help.

You can laugh at Christianity, you can mock it and ridicule it. But it works. It changes lives. I should say *Jesus Christ* changes lives. Christianity is not a religion; it's not a system; it's not an ethical idea; it's not a psychological phenomenon. It's a person. If you trust Christ, start watching your attitudes and actions because Jesus Christ is in the business of changing lives.

So, as you can see, finding my faith in Christ has been a process, beginning with hard-nosed research and growing into the experience of a changed life. It seems that many people today are eager for the experience—they want the kind of renewed life that I've found—but they are unwilling to put Christianity to the hard rational and evidential test. Maybe part of their reluctance is a hesitance to affirm that anything is absolutely true in the face of today's emphasis on tolerance and multiculturalism. Or maybe it stems from a fear that their exploration would raise doubts rather than affirm the truth of Christ's claims.

Is research a hindrance to one's faith in Christ? Not according to Edwin Yamauchi, one of the world's leading experts in ancient history. Yamauchi, who holds several degrees from Brandeis, is emphatic: "For me, the historical evidence has reinforced my commitment to Jesus Christ as the Son of God who loves us and died for us and was raised from the dead. It's that simple."[1]

Christianity is not a religion; it's not an ethical idea; it's not a psychological phenomenon. It's a person—Jesus Christ—who is in the business of changing lives.

When asked if historical New Testament scholarship had weakened his faith, ancient manuscript authority Bruce Metzger immediately replied, "It has built it. I've asked questions all my life. I've dug into the text, I've studied this thoroughly, and today I know with confidence that my trust in Jesus has been well placed . . . very well placed."[2]

Quotations such as these from two respected scholars affirm my purpose in writing this little book. I have tried to show you that the claims of Christ stand firm as solid historical facts, confirmed by the evidence of history, prophecy, and reason. Understanding the facts will give you a solid, dependable foundation to stand on as you experience Christ's claims for yourself in the kind of changed lives that I and millions of other Christians have experienced.

But in spite of the firmness of the facts and the authenticity of the experience, Christianity is not something you can shove down anyone's throat. You can't force Christ on anyone. You've got to live your life, and I've got to live mine. All of us are free to make our own decisions. All I can do is tell you what I've learned. After that, what you do is up to you.

Perhaps the prayer I prayed will help you: "Lord Jesus, I need you. Thank you for dying on the cross for me. Forgive me and cleanse me. At this very moment I trust you as Savior and Lord. Make me the type of person you created me to be. In Christ's name, Amen."

Notes

Chapter 2: What Makes Jesus So Different?

1. Augustus H. Strong, *Systematic Theology* (Philadelphia: Judson Press, 1907), 1:52.
2. Archibald Thomas Robertson, *Word Pictures in the New Testament* (New York: Harper & Brothers, 1932), 5:186.
3. Leon Morris, "The Gospel According to John," *The New International Commentary on the New Testament* (Grand Rapids, MI: Eerdmans, 1971), 524.
4. Charles F. Pfeiffer and Everett F. Harrison, eds., *The Wycliffe Bible Commentary* (Chicago: Moody, 1962), 943–44.
5. Lewis Sperry Chafer, *Systematic Theology* (Dallas: Dallas Theological Seminary Press, 1947), 5:21.
6. Robert M. Bowman and J. Ed Komoszewski, *Putting Jesus in His Place: The Case for the Deity of Christ* (Grand Rapids, MI: Kregel, 2007), 246–47.
7. Robert Anderson, *The Lord from Heaven* (London: James Nisbet, 1910), 5.
8. Henry Barclay Swete, *The Gospel According to St. Mark* (London: Macmillan, 1898), 339.
9. Irwin H. Linton, *The Sanhedrin Verdict* (New York: Loizeaux Bros., 1943), 7.
10. Charles Edmund Deland, *The Mis-Trials of Jesus* (Boston: Richard G. Badger, 1914), 118–19.

Chapter 3: Lord, Liar, or Lunatic?

1. C. S. Lewis, *Mere Christianity* (New York: Macmillan, 1960), 40–41.
2. F. J. A. Hort, *Way, Truth, and the Life* (New York: Macmillan, 1894), 207.
3. Kenneth Scott Latourette, *A History of Christianity* (New York: Harper & Row, 1953), 44, 48.
4. William E. Lecky, *History of European Morals from Augustus to Charlemagne* (New York: D. Appleton, 1903): 2:8–9.
5. Philip Schaff, *History of the Christian Church* (Grand Rapids, MI: Eerdmans, 1962), 109.
6. Philip Schaff, *The Person of Christ* (New York: American Tract Society, 1913), 94–95.
7. Clark H. Pinnock, *Set Forth Your Case* (Nutley, NJ: Craig Press, 1967), 62.

8. Gary R. Collins, quoted in Lee Strobel, *The Case for Christ* (Grand Rapids, MI: Zondervan, 1998), 147.

9. James T. Fisher and Lowell S. Hawley, *A Few Buttons Missing* (Philadelphia: Lippincott, 1951), 273.

10. C. S. Lewis, *Miracles: A Preliminary Study* (New York: Macmillan, 1947), 113.

11. Schaff, *The Person of Christ*, 97.

12. Dan Brown, *The Da Vinci Code* (New York: Doubleday, 2003), 233.

13. James A. Kliest, *The Epistles of St. Clement of Rome and St. Ignatius of Antioch*, "To the Ephesians" (Ramsey, NJ: Paulist Press, 1978).

14. Alexander Roberts, *First Apology, The Ante-Nicene Fathers,* vol. 1 (Grand Rapids, MI: Eerdmans, 1993), 184.

15. Joseph P. Smith, *St. Irenaeus: Proof of the Apostolic Preaching,* (Ramsey, NJ: Paulist Press, 1978), chap. 47.

16. Pliny, *Letters and Panegyricus*, trans. Betty Radice, Loeb Classical Library (Cambridge, MA: Harvard University Press, 1969): 10.96 (2.289).

17. J. Ed Komoszewski, M. James Sawyer, Daniel B. Wallace, *Reinventing Jesus* (Grand Rapids, MI: Kregel, 2006), 215.

Chapter 4: What about Science?

1. *The New Encyclopaedia Britannica: Micropaedia*, 15th ed., s.v. "scientific method."

2. James B. Conant, *Science and Common Sense* (New Haven, CT: Yale University Press, 1951), 25.

Chapter 5: The Challenge of the New Atheism

1. John F. Haught, *God and the New Atheism* (Louisville, KY: Westminster John Knox Press, 2008), 22.

2. Sam Harris, *Letter to a Christian Nation* (New York: Vintage Books, 2006), ix.

3. Richard Dawkins, *The God Delusion*, 2nd ed. with Preface (New York: Mariner Books, 2008), 58.

4. Christopher Hitchens, *God Is Not Great: How Religion Poisons Everything* (New York: Twelve, 2007), 122, 5.

5. From a letter to W. Graham (July 3, 1881), quoted in *The Autobiography of Charles Darwin and Selected Letters* (1892; reprint, New York: Dover, 1958).

6. Paul Davies, "What Happened Before the Big Bang?" in *God for the 21st Century*, ed. Russell Stannard (Philadelphia: Templeton Foundation Press, 2000), 12.

7. John C. Lennox, *God's Undertaker: Has Science Buried God?* (Oxford, England: Lion Hudson, 2007), 22-25.

8. Alfred North Whitehead, *Science and the Modern World* (New York: The Macmillan Company, 1925), 17.

9. Cited in John C. Lennox, *God's Undertaker*, 20.

10. Hitchens, *God Is Not Great*, 63–67.

11. Harris, *Letter to a Christian Nation*, 72.

12. Hitchens, *God Is Not Great*, 151.

13. William A. Dembski and Sean McDowell, *Understanding Intelligent Design* (Eugene, OR: Harvest House, 2008).

14. Antony Flew and Roy Abraham Varghese, *There Is a God: How the World's Most Notorious Atheist Changed His Mind* (New York: HarperCollins, 2007), 88.

15. George M. Whitesides, "Revolutions in Chemistry" (Priestly Medalist address), *Chemical & Engineering News* 85(13) (26 March 2007): 12–17, available online at http://pubs.acs.org/cen/coverstory/85/8513cover1.html (last accessed April 23, 2007).

16. Harris, *Letter to a Christian Nation*, 71.

17. Richard Dawkins, *The Blind Watchmaker* (New York: Norton, 1987), 17–18.

18. Bill Gates, *The Road Ahead* (Boulder, CO.: Blue Penguin, 1996), 228.

19. Dawkins, *The God Delusion*, 168.

20. Flew and Varghese, *There Is a God*, 132.

21. Freeman J. Dyson, *Disturbing the Universe* (New York: Harper & Row, 1979), 250.

22. Quoted in Paul Davies, *The Accidental Universe* (Cambridge: Cambridge University Press, 1982), 118.

23. Paul Davies, *Superforce: The Search for a Grand Unified Theory of Nature* (New York: Simon and Schuster, 1984), 242.

24. Stephen Hawking, *A Brief History of Time* (New York: Bantam Books, 1996), 126.

25. Walter L. Bradley, "The 'Just So' Universe," in *Signs of Intelligence*, ed. William A. Dembski and James M. Kushiner (Grand Rapids, MI.: Brazos Press, 2001), 169.

26. Roger Penrose, *The Emperor's New Mind* (New York: Oxford, 1989), 344.

27. Paul Davies, *Cosmic Jackpot* (New York: Houghton Mifflin, 2007), 149.

28. Dawkins, *The God Delusion*, 258.

29. Ibid., 35.

30. Sam Harris, *The End of Faith: Religion, Terror, and the End of Reason* (New York: W. W. Norton, 2005), 35.

31. Dinesh D'Souza, *What's So Great about Christianity* (Washington, DC: Regnery, 2007), 207.

32. Ibid., 214.

33. David Berlinski, *The Devil's Delusion: Atheism and Its Scientific Pretensions* (New York: Crown Forum, 2008), 26.

Chapter 6: Are the Bible Records Reliable?

1. Millar Burrows, *What Mean These Stones? The Significance of Archeology for Biblical Studies* (New York: Meridian Books, 1956), 52.

2. William F. Albright, *Recent Discoveries in Bible Lands* (New York: Funk and Wagnalls, 1955), 136.

3. William F. Albright, *Christianity Today*, no. 7 (18 January18 1963): 3.

4. Sir William Ramsay, *The Bearing of Recent Discovery on the Trustworthiness of the New Testament* (London: Hodder and Stoughton, 1915), 222.

5. John A. T. Robinson, *Redating the New Testament* (London: SCM Press, 1976).

6. Simon Kistemaker, *The Gospels in Current Study* (Grand Rapids, MI: Baker, 1972), 48–49.

7. A. H. McNeile, *An Introduction to the Study of the New Testament* (London: Oxford University Press, 1953), 54.

8. Paul L. Maier, *First Easter: The True and Unfamiliar Story in Words and Pictures* (New York: Harper & Row, 1973), 122.

9. William F. Albright, *From the Stone Age to Christianity*, 2nd ed. (Baltimore: John Hopkins Press, 1946), 297–98.

10. Jeffery L. Sheler, *Is The Bible True?* (New York: HarperCollins Publishers, 1999), 41.

11. Dan Brown, *The Da Vinci Code*, 231.

12. Philip Jenkins, *Hidden Gospels: How the Search for Jesus Lost Its Way* (New York: Oxford University Press, 2001), 83.

13. As quoted in Philip Jenkins's *Hidden Gospels,* 98–99.

14. Chauncey Sanders, *Introduction to Research in English Literary History* (New York: Macmillan, 1952), 143 ff.

15. F. F. Bruce, *The New Testament Documents: Are They Reliable?* (Downers Grove, IL: InterVarsity, 1964), 16.

16. Bruce Metzger, quoted in Lee Strobel, *The Case for Christ* (Grand Rapids, MI: Zondervan, 1998), 60.

17. Personal correspondence from Dan Wallace, January 6, 2003.

18. Jacob Klausner, quoted in Will Durant, *Caesar and Christ: The Story of Civilization,* pt. 3 (New York: Simon and Schuster, 1944), 557.

19. Sir Frederic Kenyon, *The Bible and Archaeology* (New York: Harper & Row, 1940), 288–89.

20. Stephen Neill, *The Interpretation of the New Testament* (London: Oxford University Press, 1964), 78.

21. Craig L. Blomberg, "The Historical Reliability of the New Testament," in William Lane Craig, *Reasonable Faith* (Wheaton, IL: Crossway, 1994), 226.

22. J. Harold Greenlee, *Introduction to New Testament Textual Criticism* (Grand Rapids, MI: Eerdmans, 1954), 16.

23. As quoted in J. Ed Komoszewski, M. James Sawyer, Daniel B. Wallace, *Reinventing Jesus,* 215.

24. Ibid., 109.

25. John Warwick Montgomery, *Where Is History Going?* (Grand Rapids, MI: Zondervan, 1969), 46.

26. Louis R. Gottschalk, *Understanding History* (New York: Knopf, 1969), 150.

27. John McRay, quoted in Strobel, *The Case for Christ,* 97.

28. Lynn Gardner, *Christianity Stands True* (Joplin, MO.: College Press, 1994), 40.

29. Norman L. Geisler, *Christian Apologetics* (Grand Rapids, MI: Baker, 1988), 316.

30. F. F. Bruce, *The New Testament Documents,* 33.

31. Lawrence J. McGinley, *Form Criticism of the Synoptic Healing Narratives* (Woodstock, MD: Woodstock College Press, 1944), 25.

32. David Hackett Fischer, *Historian's Fallacies: Toward a Logic of Historical Thought,* quoted in Norman L. Geisler, *Why I Am A Christian* (Grand Rapids, MI: Baker, 2001), 152.

33. Robert Grant, *Historical Introduction to the New Testament* (New York: Harper & Row, 1963), 302.

34. Will Durant, *Caesar and Christ,* 557.

35. Gottschalk, *Understanding History,* 161.

36. Eusebius, *Ecclesiastical History,* bk. 3, chap. 39.

37. Irenaeus, *Against Heresies,* 3.1.1.

38. Gary Habermas, *The Historical Jesus: Ancient Evidence for the Life of Christ* (Joplin, MO: College Press, 1997), 224.

39. Joseph Free, *Archaeology and Bible History* (Wheaton, IL: Scripture Press, 1964), 1.

40. F. F. Bruce, "Archaeological Confirmation of the New Testament," *Revelation and the Bible*, ed. Carl Henry (Grand Rapids, MI: Baker, 1969), 331.

41. A. N. Sherwin-White, *Roman Society and Roman Law in the New Testament* (Oxford: Clarendon Press, 1963), 189.

42. Clark H. Pinnock, *Set Forth Your Case* (Nutley, NJ: Craig Press, 1968), 58.

43. Douglas R. Groothuis, *Jesus in an Age of Controversy* (Eugene, OR: Harvest House, 1996), 39.

Chapter 7: Who Would Die for a Lie?

1. Although the New Testament does not record the deaths of these men, historical sources and long-standing tradition confirm the nature of their deaths.

2. Richard Bauckham, *Jesus and the Eyewitnesses* (Grand Rapids, MI: Eerdmans, 2006).

3. Flavius Josephus, *Antiquities of the Jews*, xx, 9:1.

4. J. P. Moreland, quoted in Lee Strobel, *The Case for Christ* (Grand Rapids, MI: Zondervan, 1998), 248.

5. Edward Gibbon, quoted in Philip Schaff, *History of the Christian Church* (Peabody, MA.: Hendrickson Publishers, 1996), chap. 3.

6. Michael Green, "Editor's Preface" in George Eldon Ladd, *I Believe in the Resurrection of Jesus* (Grand Rapids, MI: Eerdmans, 1975), vii.

7. Blaise Pascal, quoted in Robert W. Gleason, ed., *The Essential Pascal*, trans. G. F. Pullen (New York: Mentor-Omega Books, 1966), 187.

8. J. P. Moreland, quoted in Strobel, *The Case for Christ*, 246–47.

9. Michael Green, *Man Alive!* (Downers Grove, IL: InterVarsity, 1968), 23–24.

10. Quoted by J. N. D. Anderson, "The Resurrection of Christ," *Christianity Today* (29 March 1968).

11. Kenneth Scott Latourette, *A History of Christianity* (New York: Harper & Brothers Publishers, 1937), 1:59.

12. N. T. Wright, *Jesus: The Search Continues.* Transcript of this video can be read by searching for *Jesus: The Search Continues* at the Ankerberg Theological Research Institute Web site: www.johnankerberg.org.

13. Paul Little, *Know Why You Believe* (Wheaton, IL: Scripture Press, 1971), 63.

14. Herbert B. Workman, *The Martyrs of the Early Church* (London: Charles H. Kelly, 1913), 18–19.

15. Harold Mattingly, *Roman Imperial Civilization* (London: Edward Arnold Publishers, 1967), 226.

16. Tertullian, quoted in Gaston Foote, *The Transformation of the Twelve* (Nashville: Abingdon, 1958), 12.

17. Simon Greenleaf, *An Examination of the Testimony of the Four Evangelists by the Rules of Evidence Administered in the Courts of Justice* (Grand Rapids, MI: Baker, 1965), 29.

18. Lynn Gardner, *Christianity Stands True* (Joplin, MO.: College Press, 1994), 30.

19. Personal correspondence from Tom Anderson, January 6, 2003.

20. J. P. Moreland, *Scaling the Secular City* (Grand Rapids, MI: Baker, 1987),137.

21. William Lane Craig, quoted in Strobel, *The Case for Christ*, 220.

Chapter 8: What Good Is a Dead Messiah?

1. *Encyclopedia International* (New York: Grolier, 1972): 4:407.

2. Ernest Findlay Scott, *Kingdom and the Messiah* (Edinburgh: T. & T. Clark, 1911), 55.

3. Joseph Klausner, *The Messianic Idea in Israel* (New York: Macmillan, 1955), 23.

4. Jacob Gartenhaus, "The Jewish Conception of the Messiah," *Christianity Today* (13 March 1970): 8–10.

5. *Jewish Encyclopedia* (New York: Funk and Wagnalls, 1906): 8:508.

6. Millar Burrows, *More Light on the Dead Sea Scrolls* (London: Secker & Warburg, 1958), 68.

7. A. B. Bruce, *The Training of the Twelve* (Grand Rapids, MI: Kregel, 1971), 177.

8. Alfred Edersheim, *Sketches of Jewish Social Life in the Days of Christ* (Grand Rapids, MI: Eerdmans, 1960), 29.

9. George Eldon Ladd, *I Believe in the Resurrection of Jesus* (Grand Rapids, MI: Eerdmans, 1975), 38.

Chapter 9: Did You Hear What Happened to Saul?

1. *Encyclopaedia Britannica*, s.v. "Paul, Saint."

2. Jacques Dupont, "The Conversion of Paul, and Its Influence on His Understanding of Salvation by Faith," *Apostolic History and the Gospel*, ed. W. Ward Gasque and Ralph P. Martin (Grand Rapids, MI: Eerdmans, 1970), 177.

3. *Encyclopaedia Britannica*, s.v. "Paul, Saint."

4. Ibid.

5. Kenneth Scott Latourette, *A History of Christianity* (New York: Harper & Row, 1953), 76.

6. W. J. Sparrow-Simpson, *The Resurrection and the Christian Faith* (Grand Rapids, MI: Zondervan Publishing House, 1968), 185–86.

7. Dupont, "The Conversion of Paul, and Its Influence on His Understanding of Salvation by Faith," *Apostolic History and the Gospel*, 76.

8. Philip Schaff, *History of the Christian Church* (Grand Rapids, MI: Eerdmans, 1910): 1:296.

9. *Encyclopaedia Britannica*, s.v. "Paul, Saint."

10. Archibald McBride, quoted in *Chambers's Encyclopedia* (London: Pergamon Press, 1966): 10: 516.

11. Clement, quoted in Philip Schaff, *History of the Apostolic Church* (New York: Charles Scribner, 1857), 340.

12. George Lyttleton, *The Conversion of St. Paul* (New York: American Tract Society, 1929), 467.

Chapter 10: Can You Keep a Good Man Down?

1. Alexander Metherell, quoted in Lee Strobel, *The Case for Christ* (Grand Rapids, MI: Zondervan, 1998), 195–96.

2. John Dominic Crossan, *Jesus: A Revolutionary Biography* (New York: HarperOne, 1995), 145.

3. George Currie, *The Military Discipline of the Romans from the Founding of the City to the Close of the Republic*. An abstract of a thesis published under the auspices of the Graduate Council of Indiana University, 1928, 41–43.

4. A. T. Robertson, *Word Pictures in the New Testament* (New York: R. R. Smith, 1931), 239.

5. Arthur Michael Ramsey, *God, Christ and the World* (London: SCM Press, 1969), 78–80.

6. James Hastings, ed., *Dictionary of the Apostolic Church* (New York: C. Scribner's Sons, 1916): 2:340.

7. Paul Althaus, quoted in Wolfhart Pannenberg, *Jesus—God and Man*, trans. Lewis L. Wilkins and Duane A. Priebe (Philadelphia: Westminster Press, 1968), 100.

8. Paul L. Maier, "The Empty Tomb as History," *Christianity Today* (28 March 1975): 5.

9. Josh McDowell, *Evidence That Demands a Verdict* (San Bernadino, CA: Campus Crusade for Christ International, 1973), 231.

10. David Friederick Strauss, *The Life of Jesus for the People* (London: Williams and Norgate, 1879): 1: 412.

11. J. N. D. Anderson, *Christianity: The Witness of History* (London: Tyndale Press, 1969), 92.

12. John Warwick Montgomery, *History and Christianity* (Downers Grove, IL: InterVarsity, 1972), 78.

13. Jeffrey Jay Lowder, "Historical Evidence and the Empty Tomb Story" in *The Empty Tomb: Jesus Beyond the Grave*, Jeffrey Jay Lowder and Robert Price, ed. (Amherst, MA: Prometheus, 2005), 267.

14. As quoted in Lee Strobel, *The Case for the Real Jesus*, 146.

15. Stephen T. Davis, "The Counterattack of the Resurrection Skeptics," in *Philosophia Christi*, vol. 8, no. 1 (2006): 55.

16. Paul Rhodes Eddy and Gregory A. Boyd, *The Jesus Legend* (Grand Rapids: Baker Books, 2007), 142.

17. T. N. D. Mettinger, *The Riddle of Resurrection: "Dying and Rising Gods" in the Ancient Near East* (Stockholm: Almqvist and Wiksell, 2001), 221.

18. Thomas Arnold, *Christian Life—Its Hopes, Its Fears, and Its Close* (London: T. Fellowes, 1859), 324.

19. Brooke Foss Westcott, quoted in Paul E. Little, *Know Why You Believe* (Wheaton, IL: Scripture Press, 1967), 70.

20. William Lane Craig, *Jesus: The Search Continues*. Transcript of this video can be read by searching for *Jesus: The Search Continues* at the Ankerberg Theological Research Institute Web site: www.johnankerberg.org.

21. Simon Greenleaf, *An Examination of the Testimony of the Four Evangelists by the Rules of Evidence Administered in the Courts of Justice* (Grand Rapids, MI: Baker, 1965), 29.

22. Sir Lionel Luckhoo, quoted in Strobel, *The Case for Christ*, 254.

23. Frank Morison, *Who Moved the Stone?* (London: Faber and Faber, 1930).

24. George Eldon Ladd, *I Believe in the Resurrection of Jesus* (Grand Rapids, MI: Eerdmans, 1975), 141.

25. Gary Habermas and Anthony Flew, *Did Jesus Rise from the Dead? The Resurrection Debate* (San Francisco: Harper & Row, 1987), xiv.

26. Lord Darling, quoted in Michael Green, *Man Alive!* (Downers Grove, IL: InterVarsity, 1968), 54.

Chapter 11: Will the Real Messiah Please Stand Up?

1. For a more complete discussion of the Daniel 9 prophecy, see Josh McDowell, *The New Evidence That Demands a Verdict* (Nashville: Nelson, 1999), 197–201.

2. Matthew attributes the passage he quotes in 27:9-10 to the prophet Jeremiah, but the passage actually occurs in Zechariah 11:11-13. The apparent discrepancy is resolved when we understand the

organization of the Hebrew canon. Hebrew Scriptures were divided into three sections: law, writings, and prophets. Jeremiah came first in their order of prophetic books, and thus Hebrew scholars often found it an acceptable shortcut to refer to the entire collection of prophetic writings by the name of the first book—Jeremiah.

3. H. Harold Hartzler, from the foreword to Peter W. Stoner, *Science Speaks* (Chicago: Moody, 1963).

4. Stoner, *Science Speaks*, 107.

5. Ibid.

Chapter 13: He Changed My Life

1. Edwin Yamauchi, quoted in Lee Strobel, *The Case for Christ* (Grand Rapids, MI: Zondervan, 1998), 90.

2. Bruce Metzger, quoted in Strobel, *The Case for Christ*, 71.

About the Authors

Josh McDowell received a master's degree in theology from Talbot Theological Seminary in California. In 1964 he joined the staff of Campus Crusade for Christ (CCC) and eventually became an international traveling representative for the organization, focusing primarily on issues facing today's young people.

Josh has spoken to more than ten million young people in eighty-four countries, including more than seven hundred university and college campuses. He has authored or coauthored more than 110 books and workbooks with more than thirty-five million in print worldwide. Josh's most popular books are *The New Evidence That Demands a Verdict*, *Why True Love Waits*, *Right from Wrong* and the Right from Wrong workbook series.

Josh and his wife, Dottie, live in Dana Point, California, and have four grown children.

Sean McDowell is a high school teacher, speaker, and author. He graduated summa cum laude from Talbot Theological Seminary with a double master's degree in philosophy and theology. He is the author of *Ethix: Being Bold in a Whatever World*, and coauthor of *Understanding Intelligent Design* and *Evidence for the Resurrection*. Sean is also the general editor for *Apologetics for a New Generation* and *The Apologetics Study Bible for Students*.

Sean was named Educator of the Year for San Juan Capistrano in 2007–08. His apologetics training has received exemplary status from the Association of Christian Schools International. He has been a guest on radio shows such as *Focus on the Family*, *The Bible Answer Man*, *Point of View*, and *The Frank Pastore Show*. You can read Sean's blog and contact him for speaking events at http://www.seanmcdowell.org.

In April 2000, Sean married his high school sweetheart, Stephanie. They have two children, Scottie and Shauna, and live in San Juan Capistrano, California.

Share the Story.

With over 15 million copies in print, this modern classic
has introduced countless people to Jesus. Now, in this newly
updated version, Josh McDowell is joined by his son, Sean,
as they reexamine the evidence for today's generation:
Is Jesus really the Lord he claimed to be?

Available as a stand-alone book (**978-1-4143-2627-6**),
in Personal Evangelism Packs (**6 BOOKS; 978-1-4143-2628-3**),
and in Church Evangelism Packs (**30 BOOKS; 978-1-4143-3206-2**).

CP0316

Serving others until the whole world hears.

Visit **www.josh.org** for articles, discussion guides, videos, devotionals, and other resources to help you share the story of God's love.